2013

817

HAL MOORE

HAL MOORE

A Soldier Once...
And Always

MIKE GUARDIA

Casemate
Philadelphia & Oxford

Published in the United States of America and Great Britain by
CASEMATE PUBLISHERS
1950 Road, Havertown, PA 19083
and
10 Hythe Bridge Street, Oxford, OX1 2EW

ISBN 978-1-61200-207-1
Digital Edition: ISBN 978-1-61200-208-8

Cataloging-in-publication data is available from the Library of Congress and
the British Library.

Printed and bound in the United States of America.

For a complete list of Casemate titles please contact:

CASEMATE PUBLISHERS (US)
Telephone (610) 853-9131, Fax (610) 853-9146
E-mail: casemate@casematepublishing.com

CASEMATE PUBLISHERS (UK)
Telephone (01865) 241249, Fax (01865) 794449
E-mail: casemate-uk@casematepublishing.co.uk

D82016

CONTENTS

ALSO BY MIKE GUARDIA

American Guerrilla
Shadow Commander

Dedicated to the men and women of the US Armed Forces.

Lieutenant Hal Moore in his first stateside portrait, 1949. After three years in Occupied Japan, Hal returned the United States with orders to the 82nd Airborne Division at Fort Bragg, North Carolina. *The Hal Moore Collection*

INTRODUCTION

"Let us understand the situation. We are going into battle against a tough and determined enemy. I can't promise you that I will bring you all home alive, but this I swear, before you and before almighty God: that when we go into battle, I will be the first one to set foot on the field, and I will be the last to step off. And I will leave no one behind. Dead or alive, we will all come home together. So help me God."

This was the promise made by Lieutenant Colonel Harold G. "Hal" Moore to the men of 1st Battalion, 7th Cavalry on the eve of their deployment to Vietnam. On the morning of November 14, 1965, Hal Moore led the 400-man battalion against two North Vietnamese Army (NVA) regiments at the Battle of Ia Drang—one of the first major battles of the Vietnam War. Outnumbered four to one, Lieutenant Colonel Moore led his battalion to a surprising victory which claimed the lives of over 1,200 enemy soldiers. Seventy-nine Americans died in the engagement.

The Battle of Ia Drang pioneered the use of "airmobile infantry"—delivering troops into battle via helicopter. Moore himself had played a key role in developing airmobility tactics during the early 1960s. Together with journalist Joseph L. Galloway, he later wrote about his experiences at Ia Drang in the critically acclaimed book *We Were Soldiers Once . . . and Young*, which Paramount Pictures later adapted into the film *We Were Soldiers*, starring Mel Gibson.

A 1945 West Point graduate, Moore's military career began as World War II ended. After serving a three-year tour with the 11th Airborne Division in

Occupied Japan, Moore returned to the United States and then served in the Korean War. As a young captain, he fought in the Battles of Old Baldy, T-Bone, and Pork Chop Hill. Following his subsequent year-long tour in Vietnam, Moore commanded the 7th Infantry Division, forward-stationed in South Korea. At the time, the US 7th Division (like most units in the Army) suffered from race riots, illegal drug use, and gang violence. To correct these problems, Moore relieved a number of key leaders within the division and initiated a new program of training and discipline. By the end of his tenure, the division's disciplinary problems had virtually disappeared and combat readiness surged to an all-time high. Returning stateside in 1971, he assumed command of the Army Training Center at Fort Ord, California. In this capacity, he oversaw the development of several training programs for *Project VOLAR* (Volunteer Army)—the US Army's transition from a conscript-based force to an all-volunteer force. He retired as a Lieutenant General in 1977.

Like most of my fellow Millennials (i.e. those born after 1980), my introduction to Hal Moore was the film *We Were Soldiers*, which I saw on opening night in 2002. It quickly became one of my favorite films and, to this day it remains the best Vietnam War picture that I have ever seen. *We Were Soldiers* was also the first film I had seen to portray the Vietnam veteran in a positive light. For years, my generation had grown up on such fare as *Platoon*, *Full Metal Jacket*, *The Deer Hunter*, *Apocalypse Now*, and *Casualties of War*—all of which portrayed the Vietnam veteran as either malicious or mentally unstable. *We Were Soldiers*, however, was an earnest and intimate portrayal of the men who answered their country's call of duty in Southeast Asia.

In the years following the film's release, I read the books *We Were Soldiers Once . . . and Young* and *We Are Soldiers Still*. However, I was surprised to learn that no one had yet written a biography of Hal Moore himself.

At the time I began researching this book, Moore was eighty-eight years old and living quietly in Auburn, Alabama. We began our correspondence first through a series of letters and telephone interviews. Several months later, I had the opportunity to visit Hal Moore at his home, where he and I spent an entire week discussing his life and career. He graciously granted me access to his personal archives—which included a wealth of personal papers, photographs, government documents, war trophies, and *We Were Soldiers* memorabilia.

During one of our initial interviews, Moore indicated that he had three younger siblings—Betty, Bill, and Ballard—all of whom were still living. All three siblings graciously gave me their time and readily shared memories of life with their elder brother. Moore's five children—Gregory, Steven, Julie, Cecile, and David—supported me throughout every phase of this project.

Aside from *We Were Soldiers Once . . . and Young* and *We Are Soldiers Still*, other works produced by Moore include *Building a Volunteer Army: The Fort Ord Contribution*, a 139-page monograph published by the Army Center of Military History. *Building a Volunteer Army* chronicles the early years of Project VOLAR and Moore's development of the training programs therein. The After-Action Reports written by Moore give a detailed account of his units' battles in the Ia Drang Valley and Bong Son campaigns. Other primary sources included video footage from Moore's interviews at the Priztker Military Library, Texas Tech University Vietnam Studies Center, and the American Veterans Center.

I was fortunate that there was a wealth of secondary sources available for this project. Lawrence H. Johnson's seminal text, *Winged Sabers: The Air Cavalry in Vietnam*, is an authoritative account of the history of air cavalry and airmobile warfare. *Airmobility 1961–1971*, published under the *Vietnam Studies* series at the Army Center of Military History, also provides a comprehensive study of American heliborne warfare. In *Seven Firefights in Vietnam*, by John A. Cash, the entire first chapter is dedicated to the Battle of Ia Drang, while Shelby Stanton's *The 1st Cav in Vietnam: Anatomy of a Division* provided a detailed account of each brigade's operations throughout Vietnam.

For contextual clarity, I also referenced E.M. Flanagan's *The Angels: A History of the 11th Airborne Division*. Although primarily a combat history, Flanagan's work also addresses the first year of the 11th Airborne's occupation duty in post-war Japan. *This Kind of War*, by TR Fehrenbach, is perhaps the most authoritative work on the politico-military dynamics of the Korean conflict. *The United States Army in the Korean War* series, another publication from the Army Center of Military History, was an indispensible resource in building my narrative for the hilltop battles of the Korean War

I give special thanks to Hal Moore and his children for their kindness and hospitality. Without their collective help, this book may never have been written. I would also like to thank the courteous and attentive staff at the Military History Institute, the American Veterans Center, and the Copyright Clearance Center for their assistance during my research. Special thanks to Bill Walls and Pike Conway, two of Moore's childhood friends who graciously shared their memories with me. Special thanks are also reserved for Colonel David Moore (USA, ret.) and his wife, Teresa Molinari Moore, for helping me coordinate my visit to Hal Moore's home in Alabama. Finally, I would like to thank the editorial/production team at Casemate Publishers for their patience and professional support.

In a career which spanned over thirty years, Harold G. Moore proved himself to be a remarkable leader. This is his story. For he was a soldier once . . . and always.

CHAPTER ONE

EARLY YEARS

T he story of Harold Gregory Moore, Jr. begins in the foothills of southern Appalachia. Born on February 13, 1922 in Bardstown, Kentucky, "Hal" was the eldest of four children born to Harold Sr. and Mary Moore (neé Crume). At the time of Moore's birth, Bardstown was a small wisp of a community with a population of less than 4,000. Nestled deep in the highlands of the Ohio River Valley, the rural Bardstown was a perfect place for Moore to feed his adventurous spirit. Like most boys growing up in small-town Kentucky, he immersed himself in the local variety of team sports—football, basketball, and baseball. His true childhood passion, however, was always the great outdoors. From an early age, he had a near-insatiable appetite for camping, hunting, and fishing. Very often, he would disappear into the woods behind his house, pitch a tent by his favorite fishing hole, and remain out there for days before returning home to show off his latest catch.[1]

Moore's childhood home in Bardstown, Kentucky. *Photo by author*

Life in the Moore household revolved around three tenets: hard work, loyalty to the family, and devotion to the Catholic faith. The elder Moore was a strict, yet very loving father—Victorian in his principles, yet simple in his tastes. Every morning, he would rise early to attend the 6:00 a.m. Mass at the Basilica of St. Joseph. And although he never finished high school, Harold Sr. was one among the most respected insurance agents in western Kentucky. Mary was a homemaker and, by all accounts, the emotional bedrock of the family. She was a Methodist, but agreed to raise the children Catholic. Yet Harold and Mary's denominational differences never bothered them once. In fact, as Hal recalled, his mother "was more Catholic in some of her ways, as she would go to church and light candles for our family all of her life."[2]

Throughout the Great Depression, the Moores fared better than most. For even during the hardest of economic times, Hal remembered that "my father had good work and we always had plenty to eat." Hal and his siblings also took part-time jobs within the community. "I cut grass for a number of people, I caddied at the local golf course, and I worked Saturdays as a clerk at the local grocery store." And, from an early age, the young Moore possessed a remarkable fascination with all things military. Indeed, when he wasn't riding his bicycle, casting lines at the local fishing hole, or taking care of his younger siblings (Betty, Bill, and Ballard), Moore could be found at the Bardstown Public Library, devouring any book he could find on military history. He particularly enjoyed reading about the great battlefield commanders of

Snow day in Bardstown, 1937. Pictured from left to right are: Hal Moore, Bill Moore, Betty Moore, and an unidentified childhood friend. *The Bill Moore Collection*

The former campus of St. Joseph's Preparatory School in Bardstown, Kentucky, where Hal Moore graduated with the Class of 1940. The school closed its doors in 1968, following years of financial hardship and declining enrollment. *Photo courtesy of Kenny Browning*

the American Revolution and the Civil War. From George Washington to Winfield Scott, these men embodied the same values which Moore sought to maintain in his own life. And by the dawn of his teenage years, Hal knew that he had found his calling.

Aware of his son's enthusiasm for the military, Harold Sr. approached him with a suggestion that he apply to the United States Military Academy at West Point. It was 1937 and Hal was then a sophomore at St. Joseph's Preparatory School in Bardstown. The younger Moore was fascinated by West Point's legacy of leadership. Its graduates included many of the heroic leaders whom he had read about at the local library—including Ulysses S. Grant, Robert E. Lee, Stonewall Jackson, and John J. Pershing. Since its founding in 1802, West Point had been the nation's premier military academy and the primary source of commissioned officers for the US Army. A rockbound citadel ensconced on the banks of the Hudson River, West Point lay some fifty miles north of New York City. The school was renowned for its uncompromising standards of honor and discipline—and the gothic architecture of the campus complemented its reputation as one of the most rigorous schools in America.

Gaining admission to West Point, however, was no easy task. The applicant files read like a virtual "Who's Who" of America's best young scholars.

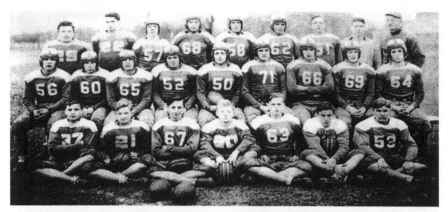

The 1938 St. Joseph's Football Team. Moore is Number 21, seated in the first row, second from the left. *St. Joseph's Alumni Association*

St.Jospeh'sgraduating class of 1940. Moore stands in the second row, second from the right. *St. Joseph's Alumni Association*

Valedictorians, National Merit Scholars, and Eagle Scouts were among the many who sought to join the Long Gray Line. Admission to the Academy was further restricted by a Congressional nomination process. A prospective cadet first had to obtain a nomination from his Congressman or Senator to be considered for admission. Moore certainly had the academic credentials, but he knew that his chances of receiving a nomination from the "backwoods of Kentucky" were slim to none.[3]

Opportunity knocked, however, on the afternoon of February 12, 1940. A seventeen-year-old Hal Moore was lying bed-ridden with pneumonia when his father came home with exciting news. Coming into the bedroom where Mary was tending to her ill son, the elder Moore wasted no time. Hal recalled that "the local representative of U.S. Senator A.B. 'Happy' Chandler had informed Dad that the senator had a patronage job opening in the Senate Book Warehouse in Washington—and it was mine if I wanted it." The pay was a mere $30 per week, ($485.71 in 2012 dollars) but to a seventeen-year-old in 1940, it was an enviable sum. His father needed an answer immediately and, if Hal accepted the job, he would be on the next train to Washington DC.[4]

Hal realized that this may have been his only chance to gain an appointment. However, he still needed to finish high school. He was currently in his last semester at St. Joseph's and only a few credits shy of graduation. But Moore's father, always one step ahead, had already spoken to the school's principal. It turned out that the principal agreed to let Hal graduate in June if he could finish the remaining credits at another school in Washington. The following morning, on Hal's eighteenth birthday, he and his father left Bardstown on the 5:00 a.m. train. "We spent the night in West Virginia and reached Washington DC on February 14 in the afternoon," Moore said.[5]

Arriving in Washington, Moore rented a room from an elderly couple, enrolled at a local night school, and made an appointment with the nearest doctor to treat his lingering pneumonia. The following day, he reported to the Senate Book Warehouse. His job consisted mostly of clerical tasks—inventorying, stocking, and shipping various titles. Mundane and repetitive as it was, Moore still embraced his job with a delightful enthusiasm. Every day, he rose from his bed in the hopes that he would find a congressman or senator with an unfilled appointment to his dream

Harold G. Moore, Sr. The elder Moore was a devout Catholic and strove to ensure that his children received the finest education. *The Ballard Moore Collection*

school. "Every month I pored over the list from the War Department of unfilled West Point appointments, and went knocking on the doors of senators and congressmen on Capitol Hill trying to persuade one of them to give me that appointment," Moore said. "I had no luck in the beginning, but I kept studying that list and walking the halls of Congress."[6]

Trolling the halls of Congress by day, Moore finished his high school credits for Algebra and English by night. That June, he returned to Bardstown to walk across the stage with his graduating class at St. Joseph's. Although he had not yet received an appointment to the Academy, Moore vowed to remain in Washington until he did. In the meantime, he continued to work at the Senate Book Warehouse and enrolled at George Washington University. Moving out of his rented room, he pledged his membership to the Kappa Sigma fraternity and became their house manager in the fall of 1940.

All the while, Moore continued his quest for a nomination to West Point. Ironically, his fortunes changed on December 7, 1941. Early that morning, the Imperial Japanese Navy launched a surprise attack on Pearl Harbor. "I was shocked, like everyone else in America," Moore said. Prior to the attack, nearly everyone had considered Japan's military an inferior force. No one had anticipated a first strike against Hawaii, much less from the Japanese. The following day, the US declared war on the Axis Powers, and "President Franklin D. Roosevelt signed legislation granting every senator and representative an additional appointment to both the Military and Naval academies."[7]

Sensing an opportunity, Hal went to Senator Chandler's office, brimming with hope that the new manpower needs would secure his nomination. Unfortunately, the senator had already given his last slot to another young man. Undeterred, Moore went to see his local congressman, Rep. Ed Creal (4th District, Kentucky). Creal sheepishly told him that he, too, had just given away his last slot. Creal did, however, have an open appointment to the US Naval Academy, and offered it to Moore.

Although Moore had no desire to go to Annapolis, he thanked Creal for the appointment. But suddenly, Moore had an idea: "What if I can find another Congressman who would appoint me to West Point in exchange for Representative Creal's Naval Academy appointment?" Creal was surprised by the young Moore's proposal, but agreed to it if Hal could find a congressman willing to make the swap. Hal soon found his way into the office of Congressman Eugene E. Cox, representing the 2nd District of Georgia. "I walked into his office and I was greeted by his secretary, a Mrs. J.C. Robinson," Moore

An aerial photograph of West Point at mid-century. It was often said, "If God is an American, He resides in the chapel above West Point." *West Point Photo*

New cadets line up for equipment issue on R-Day, 1942. These new cadets are wearing the standard-issue gray trousers, affectionately known as "Plebe skins." *The Hal Moore Collection*

Under the watchful eye of their cadre, the new cadets march to their swearing-in ceremony, July 15, 1942. *West Point Photo*

recalled. "She showed me into his office and I asked the Congressman if he would swap my Naval Academy appointment." Impressed by the young man's tenacity, Moore left that day with an appointment from the 2nd District of Georgia.[8]

In the summer of 1942, the new cadets arrived at West Point in two waves. The first contingent arrived on July 1, the second on July 15, making Moore's class the largest in West Point's young history. The cadets' first day was called Reception Day, or "R-Day." It marked the beginning of a strenuous indoctrination known as Cadet Basic Training, or "Beast Barracks," as it was commonly known. Although exclusively for West Point cadets, Beast Barracks largely resembled the Basic Training program of the Regular Army.

Most West Point graduates remember their R-Day as a blur of savage putdowns, dreadful stares, close calls with heat exhaustion, and the constant reminder that "I *wanted* to come to West Point." For Hal Moore, R-Day certainly lived up to its chaotic reputation.

He arrived at the Academy with the second wave of incoming cadets on July 15, 1942. Scurrying off the train at the West Point depot, Moore disembarked with nearly 500 other new cadets, all eager to begin their journey into officership. His classmates came from all over the country, most of them from small towns which he had never heard of: Maxwell, Texas; Copley, Ohio; and

Florence, Alabama, among others. They represented nearly every walk of life. Some were fresh out of high school while others, like Moore, had a few years of college under their belts. Some had given up trade careers in carpentry, machinery, and electrical work to try their hand at soldiering. Others had been enlisted men who traded their chevrons for cadet gray. Whatever their background, they all came with the aspiration to become officers and fight the Axis Powers.

Hal never forgot the first noncommissioned officer he met on R-Day. "When my group of soon-to-be cadets pulled into the train station we were met by a stone-faced, spit-shined sergeant with a pencil-thin mustache resplendent in Cavalry hat, Cavalry riding boots, and bloused riding breeches. His look implied that he had measured us, just as he had measured thousands like us before, and we did not for an instant impress him. His name fit him as well as those gleaming Cavalry riding boots: Master Sergeant Bonebrake. We fell into something like a formation and Bonebrake marched us up the hill and into the complex of imposing gray granite buildings brooding on the slopes and plain high above the Hudson River. There was a sense of ageless permanence, a majesty if you will, about that place, and a cold, powerful, unbending, relentless, no-nonsense authority. Master Sergeant Bonebrake fit in perfectly with the place and the weight of its history and those thick gray granite walls."[9]

Every summer during Beast Barracks, the junior and senior-year cadets assumed the role of drill sergeants, instructing the new cadets in military matters. When Bonebrake handed off Moore to his cadet instructors, the strenuous journey of Beast Barracks began. All at once, Hal's new name was "Mister."

"Get those shoulders back, Mister!"

"Hey Mister, quit looking around!"

"What do you think you're doing, Mister?!"

"MISSTERRR!"

Then came the seemingly endless drill and marching commands: "Attention! Left Face! Right Face! Forward March! At Ease!"—and very little of the latter. Soon thereafter, Moore would learn the sacred "Four Responses" which every new cadet had to use whenever he was addressed by an upperclassman. A new cadet's responses were limited to: "Yes sir," "No sir," "No excuse, sir," and "Sir, I do not understand."

After the crash course in military honorifics and close-order drill, Moore and his comrades were hoarded into the Mess Hall. Seated ten to a table, Moore and the other new arrivals had to sit at a rigid posture of attention. Except for giving or receiving food, they were not allowed to look anywhere except for their plate. They could lift their utensils to their mouths only at a ninety-degree angle and were limited to three chews per bite. At the head of the table sat a senior-year cadet known as the Table Commandant. His job, as far as Moore was concerned, was to make the meal miserable for every new cadet at his table. The table commandants were notorious for scrutinizing their younger cadets' every move—anxiously awaiting the chance to correct any breech of table etiquette.

Moore soon discovered that the cadets were not referred to as freshmen, sophomores, juniors, and seniors. Instead, they were referred to, respectively, as Fourth Class, Third Class, Second Class, and First Class cadets. Traditionally, the Fourth Classmen were known as "Plebes," a derivative of the word *Plebian*—referring to the lowest class of Roman society. Third Classmen were called "Yearlings"—a term used to describe a year-old farm animal. The Second Classmen were "Cows," but the origin of that term remains in obscurity. The most likely explanation was that, in years past, the cadets had no leave until after Yearling year. Thus, when the rising Second Classmen returned from their summer furlough, it was heralded as "the cows coming home." The First Classmen's nickname was merely an abbreviation: "Firstie."

Throughout Beast Barracks, Moore learned the fundamentals of soldier-

Hal Moore, far right, and his friends during their summer training at Camp Popolopen, summer 1943. *The Hal Moore Collection*

Moore and his classmates receive training on an amphibious vehicle (top) and the anti-tank gun (bottom) during Yearling Maneuvers, 1943. *The Hal Moore Collection*

ing: rifle marksmanship, patrolling, hand grenades, and the proper technique of shining shoes. "By August, we had been to the firing range, run the obstacle course, taken the physical efficiency tests, learned to prepare a 40-pound pack with bedroll, and demonstrated skill in hand-to-hand combat." Moore remembered that the high point for him during Beast Barracks "was firing EXPERT on the M-1 rifle with the top score in the company and being given a pint of vanilla ice cream by my Squad Leader.

"Also, early on in Beast Barracks, I discovered a safe haven—the Cath-

The Moore family on Bill's Eighth Grade Graduation Day, June 1943. Pictured from left to right: Hal Moore, Betty Moore, Harold Sr., Mary, Ballard, and Bill. Bill would go on to play football at Notre Dame and young Ballard would become a world-class tennis champion and Olympic coach. *The Bill Moore Collection*

olic Rectory. . . . I was a frequent visitor there and attended Mass often." Hal often said that his religious beliefs were his greatest source of strength during those tough times. He formed a close friendship with the Rector, Monsignor George Murdock, and the two often prayed together. Whenever his schedule permitted, Hal would slip away to the sanctuary for Daily Mass.[10]

Beast Barracks culminated with the so-called "Plebe Maneuvers" at Pine Camp (present-day Fort Drum) near Watertown, New York. It was a week-long field exercise which introduced Plebes to the art of bivouacking and how to maneuver at the squad and platoon level. Upon their return to West Point, "we regrouped into new companies formed as the Corps grew from one to two regiments to accommodate our large class." Moore found himself assigned to Company C-1 (C Company, First Regiment). "Beast Barracks had come to an end. It was time to start the academic year."[11]

Although Moore excelled in English and History, he admitted that "I was so dumb in mathematics—particularly algebra, differential equations, and solid geometry . . . but I managed through." By October, he recalled that "my name was on the list of cadets severely 'deficient' in grades in solid geometry and advanced algebra"—meaning that he was in danger of flunking out if his grades did not improve. Fearful of losing what he had worked so hard to achieve, Hal said that "I was glued to my advanced math textbooks every

The Corps of Cadets assemble for parade, December 1943. *The Hal Moore Collection*

night from 7:30 p.m. until lights out at 11:00 p.m.—and after lights out I moved to the nearby restroom down the hall from my room," where Moore sat on a toilet studying by the dim light of a 40-watt bulb. Plowing through his textbooks until 1:00 or 2:00 in the morning, Hal knew that even if "I didn't understand the advanced, arcane math and bewildering engineering, physics, and chemistry, I could at least memorize the procedures."[12]

As if the academics weren't trying enough, Moore also had to adjust to the rigors of Plebe life. Every day brought a new trial as the upperclassmen, invoking some contrived rite of passage, would harass Moore by making him recite the various topics of Plebe Knowledge. The so-called "Plebe Knowledge" was a collection of facts and folklore about West Point which every Plebe had to memorize and be ready to recite at any given moment. It covered a variety of topics—some of which were useful (the technical specifications of an M-1 rifle) while others were downright trivial (the number of gallons in nearby Lusk Reservoir). "We found the world of a Plebe to be one of survival. Once we could spout off the mandatory Plebe Knowledge, recite all the particular items given to us by upperclassmen . . . and along the way, provide a new joke . . . we usually stayed out of trouble."[13]

One facet of the Plebe system that Moore didn't mind, however, was the daily recitation from the *New York Times*. The newspaper was delivered to the cadets every morning, and a Plebe was often required to recite the day's

Father Murdock, the Catholic Rector at West Point and Hal Moore's spiritual mentor. *West Point photo*

headlines for the upperclassmen. This gave Moore a chance to read about what was happening on the front lines in Europe and the Pacific. After some initial setbacks in North Africa, Moore was glad to hear that the Allied forces were once again on the offensive. In the Pacific, the US Navy had won a decisive victory at Midway and the Army Air Forces were pounding away at the Solomon Islands.

The stories that interested him the most, however, were the ones discussing a new type of warfare—*airborne infantry*. During World War II, American airborne forces fell into two categories: parachute infantry and glider infantry. Parachute infantry, as the name implied, delivered troops into battle via parachute. Military equipment—including rations, radios, and even Jeeps—could also be fitted with parachutes for insertion into a combat zone. Glider infantry, on the other hand, placed troops into a 13-man glider which would fly behind the tether of a towing aircraft. Once the glider reached its designated landing zone, or LZ, it would detach from the tether and sail to the ground.

That fall, Hal and his classmates received some unexpected good news. The Academy's curriculum had been accelerated to three years instead of four. "No longer were we the Class of 1946; we were now the new Class of 1945!" Rumors abounded that the curriculum might be accelerated even further—perhaps to as little as eighteen months—as it had been during World War I. However, nothing came of it. Moore later discovered that even though the curriculum had been shortened by a year, "the total hours of instruction actually increased." To accommodate the new course acceleration, West Point graduated *two* classes in 1943. The original Class of 1943 accelerated to become the "Class of January 1943" while the previous Class of 1944 became the "Class of June 1943."[14]

Hal Moore made it through Plebe Year by the skin of his teeth. It was, as he called it, "an academic trip from hell." He survived his midterms and finals, "but the distressing experience of struggling for weeks to get pro [i.e. proficient] and stay pro—knowing the ominous results if not, profoundly affected me. From then on, I led an unbalanced life at the Academy [i.e. few extracurricular activities and a lot of studying]." Moore ended his Plebe Year with a 10-day furlough and a chance to get some much needed rest. But, "before we knew it, we were back at West Point for a summer of military training at Camp Popolopen.[15]

"By the summer of 1943, American and British forces had emerged victorious in North Africa and Sicily while in the Pacific theater our Allied Forces had launched the long campaign back, starting with the seizure of Guadalcanal the previous fall. We were well aware that our military training was helping to prepare us to lead men somewhere in one of those theaters of war. We fired many weapons, learned to drive tanks and other military vehicles, and participated in maneuvers culminating with a second trip to Pine Camp [where they had done Plebe Maneuvers the previous summer]."

Returning to West Point for another year of academics, Moore saw several of his classmates sign up for flight training. Before the US Air Force became its own branch, a large number of West Pointers could enroll in the "Air Cadet" program during their second year at the Academy. Their summer training took them to flight schools across the country—Arkansas, Oklahoma, Texas, and nearby Stewart Field in New Windsor, New York.

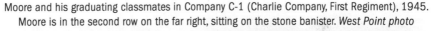

Moore and his graduating classmates in Company C-1 (Charlie Company, First Regiment), 1945. Moore is in the second row on the far right, sitting on the stone banister. *West Point photo*

"The academic year brought on a new array of more complicated subjects. One sometimes wondered what calculus, electrical engineering, and thermodynamics had to do with becoming an officer. However, the study of Caesar's campaigns, Napoleon's conquests, and Jackson's Shenendoah Valley campaign did seem more relevant." Every Wednesday, Moore and his classmates had the opportunity to watch the latest *Staff Combat Film Report*, shown in the Chemistry Lab. "These vividly brought home what we were preparing ourselves to do. The scenes of fighting in both the Pacific and Europe gave us a contrast of environments as well as a better understanding of the enemies we would be facing." Sobering as they were, Hal knew that these films portrayed combat more realistically than any newspaper, radio, or movie newsreel. That spring, the Class of 1944 graduated on June 6—simultaneous with the D-Day landings in Europe. The cadets of '45 were thrilled to hear about the invasion of Normandy, but "we wondered whether there would be any war left for us."

That summer, Moore and his classmates "took a look at the real world of tactics and techniques at Army basic training centers." Meanwhile, he kept himself abreast of the happenings in Europe and the Pacific. During the invasion of Normandy, the Allied airborne operations hadn't gone as planned—several units had missed their drop zones and become scattered over the landscape. Their hasty re-group, however, had helped to secure the Allies' toehold on the Continent until finally the German cordon collapsed and the Allies advanced headlong across Northern France toward Belgium, the Netherlands, and the border of the Reich itself. Meanwhile, in the Pacific, the "island hopping" campaign had captured Tarawa, Tinian, and Saipan. From these news reports, one thing was certain: the Allies were tightening their noose around Germany and Japan.

"On returning to the Academy, we all began the final year in earnest. Military history, in particular fascinated us, helping us to relate the various campaigns of the past to those ongoing in Europe and the Pacific." That fall, Moore was delighted to see the Army football team go through an undefeated season. The 1944 Army-Navy game was held in Baltimore, and the Corps of Cadets had initially been promised a train ride for the event. In an unexpected turn of events, however, Moore and his classmates were marched down to the West Point ferry dock and boarded the USS *Uruguay*, a troop transport fresh from the European theater. From there, "we sailed down the Hudson and out to sea for two days, escorted by what seemed to be a major portion of the US Navy, into the harbor of Baltimore. The media remained unaware of the trip. Can you imagine what would have happened had a German submarine sunk the ship with the entire Corps of Cadets on board?" The cruise, however, was well worth it—Army defeated Navy 23 to 7. "The team was declared the National Champions and many members were named All Americans." For the Corps of Cadets, it was the perfect end to a perfect season.

Meanwhile, the Allied offensive in Europe had stalled in the face of a German counterattack in the Ardennes forest, which history would term the Battle of the Bulge. "Maybe the war in Europe would wait for us after all." But soon, the Allied offensive was back on track and by February 1945, the Allies had penetrated deep into the Fatherland. With the Americans closing in from the west and the Soviets from the east, a frantic Adolf Hitler committed suicide on April 30, 1945. One week later, the German Army surrendered and the news of V-E Day rang throughout the world. But even though the war in Europe had ended, the Japanese refused to quit the fight.

"One of the highlights of winding down First Class year was ordering our officer uniforms. We had frequent discussions about the various companies that came to show us their wares. What a thrill to be able to select everything we would wear after graduating. Then came the question of branch assignment for the Ground Cadets." By this time, the Air Cadets had been carted off to Stewart Field for advanced pilot training. From there, they would earn their wings and decide whether to become bomber or fighter pilots. "The authorities set up a quota system for each branch and allowed assignments by individual choice based on academic standing."[16]

Branch selection was a nerve-racking experience for the young Cadet Moore. During his three years at the Academy, he had frittered away at his textbooks only to land in the bottom fifteen percent of his class. He desperately wanted to branch Infantry, but feared that the branch would fill its quota on the higher-ranking cadets before he had a chance to make his selection. The First Class cadets were hoarded into an auditorium and, "as each of our names was called off in order of merit, we selected a branch until that branch quota was filled, thereby forcing the next classmate to his second choice." Moore heard each of his classmates call out their choice:

"Infantry!"

"Field Artillery!"

"Engineers!"

Hal Moore's graduation portrait, 1945. His inscription in the West Point yearbook read: "Untouched by the machinations of the T.D. [Tactical Department] and Academic Departments, Hal never wasted a week-end with inactivity. The casual consistency with which he escorted beautiful young ladies remained a continual source of amazement to his classmates, but as often as not Saturday afternoon found Hal heading for the nearest fishing hole with his favorite tackle. He is ever ready to forsake his more serious pursuits for the harmony of the nearest barber shop quartet or for the joy of an all-day ski trip."
West Point photo

Fortunately, there were several infantry slots remaining when the announcer made his way down the list to "Moore, Harold G."

"Infantry!" Moore cried out.

"Finally, June Week and Graduation arrived . . . family and friends gathered to participate in its many events." However, one of Moore's fellow cadets was nearly excluded from the company's end-of-year celebration. A week before graduation, the First Classmen in Moore's cadet company held a meeting to discuss plans for a company picnic. During that meeting, a few of Moore's classmates suggested that Cadet Ernie Davis and his family not be invited. "Davis was one of three black cadets at West Point in the early 1940s and he was in the Cadet Company I was in." Disgusted, Hal stood up and said that he would boycott the company picnic if Davis and his family were not invited. "Quickly, things were reversed and Davis and family attended with our other classmates and guests."[17]

Finally, on June 5, 1945, Hal Moore walked across the stage and received his diploma from General Omar Bradley, the famed commander of the US Twelfth Army Group. "Tossing our caps into the air, we realized that the Class of 1945 had made it. Now Second Lieutenants and leaving [West Point] behind, we sallied forth to take on the world."

CHAPTER TWO

THE MILITARY LIFE

H al Moore often said that "my military career began as World War II was ending." Indeed, by Graduation Day, Germany had surrendered, the Führer was dead, and the Japanese were preparing to make their last stand in the Pacific. One by one, the enemy strongholds on Tarawa, Saipan, Iwo Jima, and Okinawa collapsed under the power of Allied offensives. But as Americans celebrated V-E Day, and the Allies continued their "island

The newly-minted Lieutenant Moore (center) relaxes with fellow classmates William Combs and Jim Herbert in San Francisco, 1945. Moore departed San Francisco Bay for the Philippine Islands, to a replacement depot where he volunteered for occupation duty in 11th Airborne Division. *The Hal Moore Collection*

hopping" campaign, the newly commissioned Lieutenant Moore celebrated another victory. After three years of academic tribulation, he was proud to say that "I graduated at the top . . . of the bottom fifteen percent of my class."[18]

With Germany out of the war, the US began sending more of its personnel to the Pacific. Like many of his classmates, Hal received orders to the Far East Command. His first place of duty, however, would be the Infantry Officer Basic Course at Fort Benning, Georgia. After six weeks of learning the fundamentals of platoon leadership, "I volunteered for the jump school at Fort Benning." The Army had established several jump schools during the war, but Fort Benning remained the primary hub for airborne training. Unfortunately, "they only had openings for about twenty-five officers during that cycle, and a lot of my classmates had also volunteered for jump school. They only took the top-ranking cadets, and I was not selected because I was way down at the bottom of my class." Disappointed, but not dejected, Hal Moore loaded his bags onto a train westbound for San Francisco—where a troop ship waited to take him to one of the many replacement depots scattered throughout the Pacific.[19]

Meanwhile, Japan's war machine slowly ground to a halt. In June 1945, the Imperial Japanese Army fought its last losing battle on the island of Ok-

Hal Moore (left) and William Combs at the "tent city" replacement depot north of Manila, Philippine Islands, 1945. As World War II had ended, life at the depot was exceedingly boring. *The Hal Moore Collection*

inawa. But even as the Allies closed in on the main archipelago, the Japanese refused to quit. Wanting to bring this destructive conflict to an end, and well aware of the bloodbath which would follow an invasion of the Japanese homeland, President Harry Truman made a profound, yet difficult decision: the atomic bomb would make its debut over the Empire of Japan.

Following the nuclear devastations of Hiroshima and Nagasaki, the Japanese government finally lost its will to fight. On August 14, 1945, Emperor Hirohito broadcasted a pre-recorded radio speech announcing his nation's unconditional surrender. He instructed all Imperial troops to lay down their arms and to cooperate with the newly arriving occupation force. Finally, on September 2, in a ceremony held aboard the USS *Missouri*, a Japanese delegation signed the official document of surrender. With the stroke of a pen, the great World War II had finally come to an end.

Meanwhile, on the other side of the Pacific, twenty-three-year-old Lieutenant Moore boarded a troop ship in San Francisco Bay. Its destination, as he found out, was the Philippine Islands—to a replacement depot north of Manila. Hal began the voyage with mixed feelings: he was glad that the US had won, but slightly disappointed that he had missed the fight. Still, the

Moore stands in front of the 11th Airborne Division's jump school near Tokyo. After five qualifying jumps from a C-47 aircraft, Moore earned his wings and reported to the 187th Glider Infantry Regiment based in Hokkaido. *The Hal Moore Collection*

A panoramic view of Camp Crawford, headquarters of the 187th Glider Infantry Regiment.
The Hal Moore Collection

thought of going to war had been hauntingly real. "I personally knew up-perclassmen who were killed in action," he said. "We were under no illusions what we were headed for. I probably would have been killed jumping into Japan, because everyone had been issued pitchforks to attack paratroopers."[20]

After a two-week voyage, Moore disembarked at Manila Bay and settled into the replacement depot. It was nothing more than a "tent city," and Moore remembered that "I stayed there with a bunch of other second lieutenants from colleges all over the country." Because the war had ended, life at the depot was decidedly boring. The lieutenants in Moore's company passed the time by playing cards, writing letters, and sharing gripes that they had missed out on World War II.

One day, however, Moore and his friends were visited by a personnel of-ficer taking volunteers for the various divisions assigned to occupation duty. Moore remembered that these units included the 24th Infantry Division, the Americal Division, and the 1st Cavalry Division, "but then I heard about the 11th Airborne Division," he said, "and that they had a jump school just north of Tokyo." Moore quickly volunteered and was on a plane to Tokyo the fol-lowing morning.

The 11th Airborne had one of the most celebrated histories of any divi-sion in World War II. Activated in 1943 at Camp Mackall, North Carolina, the 11th Airborne had participated in the liberation of Luzon and the Raid of Los Baños. After the Japanese surrender, the division had been assigned to occupation duty on the northern half of Honshu (the main island) and on Hokkaido, the northernmost prefecture of the Japanese archipelago. After establishing its first command post at the Atsugi Airfield, the division parceled its regiments into camps near the cities of Hakodate, Morioka, and Sapporo.

As Moore boarded the plane to Tokyo, he wondered how the Japanese would greet him and his fellow GIs. From US newsreels and newspapers, he had learned of the atrocities carried out by the Rising Sun. Given the savagery of their conduct, many wondered if the Japanese truly intended to abide by their surrender, or if a few "dead-enders" would continue to fight against the Allied occupation.

Landing in Tokyo, however, Moore and his comrades discovered a hauntingly different picture: the Japanese *avoided* the Americans at all costs. Some even refused to make eye contact. Others simply ran in the opposite direction if approached by a US serviceman. One paratrooper also noticed that there were no women in sight. The few women who did sneak out into the daylight "had on baggy clothes to hide any female identification. Evidently, the Japs expected us to come in raping and looting as they always did."[21]

One of Moore's fellow paratroopers, WC Kitchen, remembered an incident where he was stopped by a Japanese officer and asked, "Why don't you rape and loot and burn? We would." Kitchen just looked at the man in disbelief. "That man was genuinely puzzled by our actions," he said. "I am ashamed to tell you what an inadequate reply I gave to that man. What an opportunity I had to tell him about our God and His laws, about our traditions . . . all we wanted was peace and respect and we would do the same for others, even our enemies. Well, I mumbled something about 'we just don't do things like that.' And that was the end of it."[22]

The 11th Airborne's jump school was three weeks long, and Hal loved every minute of it. The first week was spent learning the inner workings of the parachute and practicing parachute landing falls, or PLFs. From atop a two-foot-high platform, these paratroopers-in-training would jump and land on the ground with their feet and legs together, and then roll their bodies in the direction of the fall. A paratrooper had to land on the ground this way to avoid breaking his legs.

By the end of the course, every student had to make five qualifying jumps from a C-47 aircraft. Lining up along the inside of the fuselage, Moore and

The archway at the entrance of Camp Crawford in Sapporo, Hokkaido, 1946. *The Hal Moore Collection*

his fellow paratroops would hook their "static lines" to an overhead wire which ran the length the plane. The static line was generally a fifteen-foot cord attached to the parachute on a trooper's back. Once the trooper jumped from the plane, the static line would extend until taught, at which point it would deploy the parachute from its pack as the trooper continued falling towards the ground. Humorously, Hal remembered that his Tokyo jump school class included "several of us who were dumb enough not to be selected for the jump school at Fort Benning."[23]

Pinning on his coveted airborne wings, Moore received orders to the 187th Glider Infantry Regiment at Camp Crawford, just outside Sapporo, the prefectural capital of Hokkaido. It was November 1945 when he arrived at the regimental headquarters and was assigned to E Company, 1st Battalion. Meeting his platoon, however, Moore wondered if his new charges would take him seriously. Aside from a few replacements, they were all combat veterans, some of whom had been with the unit since Camp Mackall. They had been awarded Purple Hearts, Silver Stars, and bore the heralded wreaths of the Combat Infantryman Badge. And the fresh-faced Lieutenant Moore now had the monumental task of gaining their trust and respect. Nevertheless, Moore handled their first meeting with a surprising ease. "Hello," he told them. "I'm your platoon leader. I'll do the best I can and I expect the same from you."[24]

Unfortunately, Moore would only command this platoon for three weeks. By the time he arrived at Camp Crawford, "there were very few captains," he said. "They were all being discharged." Indeed, most of the captains in Moore's unit were either graduates of Officer Candidate School or had earned battlefield commissions. Now that the war was over, their obligations to Uncle Sam had ended and they were eager to return to civilian life. Thus, "after three weeks, I was suddenly a company commander! That was a great challenge for a second lieutenant with no combat experience and only five qualifying jumps."[25]

Moore remembered that it was an interesting time to be in the Army. "I was a company commander, and by then the companies were very small because so many of the soldiers were getting out." By now, the Japanese no longer feared their American occupiers. However, the GIs—excited that the war was over and with little else to keep them busy—often ventured into town, got drunk, and engaged in colorful antics which the local Japanese didn't find amusing. Policing his soldiers "was a hell of a problem," Moore said, "because all they were interested in was drinking the Japanese beer and screwing the Japanese women." The Japanese had no societal hang-ups about sex—and the American GIs took full advantage of it. Several soldiers even had Japanese girlfriends in the local towns. During that first year of the occupation, it wasn't unusual for the MPs to pick up a handful of GIs from a drunken caper, or for a soldier to miss his morning formation because he had overslept at the local brothel.[26]

A travel guide highlighting the sights of Hokkaido. Moore purchased the booklet upon his arrival in Sapporo. *The Hal Moore Collection*

Nevertheless, Hal knew that many of his men were leaving the military and he didn't want to tie them up within the Army's legal system. Thus, whenever one of his troopers got picked up by the MPs, or took one too many romantic liaisons in Sapporo, Hal devised a simpler yet more creative way to punish them. "My punishment for them was to go running with me." Moore was an excellent runner and said "I could run five to eight miles without breaking a sweat!" His punitive running routes would go around Camp Crawford and into the trails of the mountains surrounding the post. "And I would run these sons of bitches until they puked all over the ground." Unmoved by the vomiting, Moore would tell them to "get up off the ground and keep run-

187th Infantry Regimental Headquarters, Camp Crawford, 1946. *The Hal Moore Collection*

Hal Moore's room, 10-A, at the Bachelor Officer Quarters. Pictured on the left is a Japanese orderly, one of several employed by Camp Crawford. *The Hal Moore Collection*

THE MILITARY LIFE • 39

ning!" When the exhausted trooper finally hobbled across the finish line, Moore would stand over him and say "you going to behave yourself now?" Through spurts of vomiting, the soldier would let out a muffled "Yes sir." Any soldier who went for a punitive run with Hal Moore never made trouble for him again.[27]

Although the post-World War II drawdown left the regiment with few resources, Moore still found time to do his core competency training. "I did a lot of parachute jumping," Moore said, especially during the winter. The harsh winters in Hokkaido normally brought several feet of snow to the drop zone, and the paratroopers would have to jump wearing Russian-style winter caps and "bear-claw" snowshoes. For the 187th it was great training for arctic warfare under conditions which couldn't be easily duplicated back in the US.

The snow also gave Moore an opportunity to try his hand at skiing. During his first year in Hokkaido, the 187th started a regimental cross-country skiing team. "We got every Wednesday and Saturday afternoon off from work," Hal said, and during that time, "I found this Japanese guy who had coached the Japanese Nordic Ski Team [before the war]." Taking the young American lieutenant under his wing, the Japanese expert taught Moore how to perfect his skiing technique. Aside from parachuting, these cross-country ski trips were the most fun he had while stationed in Japan.

Hal remembered that the ski instructor and some of his friends "would take me with them all over northern Japan and we would ski cross-country. I skied with a backpack, arctic sleeping bag, air mattress, and food. At night-time, we would dig a snow cave and you'd crawl in it . . . blow up the air mattress . . . and sleep in the arctic sleeping bag with nothing but your skivvies [underwear] because if you slept in your clothes, your sweat would freeze to your body." Moore was even offered a chance to compete at the 1948 Olympics. The 1940 and 1944 Olympics had been canceled because of World War II, and the Summer Games were set to resume in 1948. Veterans from across the globe were entering the preliminary competitions, but Moore declined the offer—he wanted to stay with his troops.[28]

Moore was often surprised by the hospitality of the Japanese people. As their initial fears of the American occupation faded away, Moore found them to be the most pleasant and sociable people that he had ever met. "The Emperor told them to be very hospitable to Americans, and they were." At times, he even felt as though his occupation duty was more of a goodwill tour. "I made friends with a lot of the Japanese people and they would invite me into their homes for dinner, which consisted of rice and water. I learned enough Japanese to get around, but I could never read the characters."[29]

The occupation duty did, however, bring some very unpleasant run-ins with the Japanese. One of the more unsavory aspects of Hal's duty included processing the Japanese repatriates and POWs coming back into Hokkaido. As Japan's conquered territory returned to Allied control, the Imperial troops and Japanese colonists living there were boarded onto ships and taken back to Japan. Stung by their defeat, and having lost everything in the war, these repatriated Japanese were timid, despondent, and sometimes combative with their American handlers. Nearly all of them were sick and many suffered from diseases they had gotten en route to the mainland.

After seven months as a company commander, Hal Moore suddenly became Camp Crawford's chief construction officer. "There was a lieutenant colonel with the Army Corps of Engineers who was in charge of the money, plans, and supervision of building Camp Crawford. And when he rotated out, guess who became the new camp construction officer? Me. And I was responsible for $8,000,000! (nearly $93,000,000 in 2012 dollars)" It was an enormous responsibility for a young lieutenant. Hal Moore, with no experience in construction, had to finish what a lieutenant colonel had started in building a camp "that housed the entire 187th Regiment, two artillery batteries, the 11th Airborne Division headquarters, and the replacement depot."[30]

But just as he had done before, Hal took on the new challenge with enthusiasm. The contractors for the building project were local Hokkaido natives and Moore used the opportunity to practice the Japanese language which he had learned. At first, the contractors "didn't know that I could understand what they were saying"—they would discuss the technical matters of building the camp—"but they eventually caught on that I could understand." Moore remembered that these contractors, Hirata and Torchy, were a pleasure to work with. "I had a great time building that camp," he said. His construction projects included "an Officer's Club, an NCO Club, an Enlisted Man's Club, a gymnasium, a football stadium, and a few barracks."[31]

As Moore's construction work began to wind down, he ventured into downtown Sapporo where one day he met a man named Yamada, "who had a kennel of Japanese war dogs . . . bona-fide German shepherds." It turned out that they had been shipped to Japan from Nazi Germany to use as military dogs for the Kempai Tai (the Japanese military police). One of Yamada's dogs had just given birth to a litter of pups, and Moore—quite the dog

Above: The Memorial Day Parade through downtown Sapporo, 1946. *The Hal Moore Collection*

Right: Hal Moore and Andy Gatsis in Hokodate, Hokkaido, May 1947. Gatsis, one of Moore's closest friends from the Academy, had the dubious distinction of being "The Goat" – the last ranking man in his graduating class at West Point. *The Hal Moore Collection*

Left: Parachuting over the drop zone near Hokodate, Japan. The hand-drawn arrow points to Moore's position among the other paratroopers. *The Hal Moore Collection*

Below: Parachute jump over Sapporo. During these jumps, the Japanese civilians would point to the sky and shout "Rakkasans"— translated "falling umbrellas." The term eventually became the 187th's regimental motto. *The Hal Moore Collection*

lover—adopted one of the male pups and named him "Butch."

Taking his new friend back to Camp Crawford, Butch quickly became a favorite among Moore's soldiers. "I taught that dog how to sit, how to stand, and how to speak." Butch also proved to be quite a hunting dog. Between his parachute jumps, ski expeditions, and building projects, Moore often went duck hunting with friends. On every trip, Butch would come along, his head and tongue hanging out the side of the jeep as it sped along the country trail. Every night, Butch would sleep at the foot of his master's bed at the Bachelor Officers' Quarters. And when Hal finally returned to the United States in 1948, Butch came too. "I took him down to Honshu where we boarded a plane to San Francisco," Moore said. It took a long-winded fight with the airport staff to allow Butch on the plane, but when Hal boarded with his canine companion, "everybody on the airplane fell in love with that dog."[32]

Suddenly, in the spring of 1948, Hal's regular routine of occupation duty was interrupted by an urgent communiqué from Washington. An Air Force utility aircraft had crash-landed somewhere in the jungles of Indonesia. Moore's regiment was called upon to assemble a platoon of volunteers for a mission to recover the crew's remains. Excited at the prospect of deploying on a "real-world" mission, Moore immediately volunteered.

However, this would not be a simple rescue mission. Moore and his team of volunteers would parachute into the jungle and their "small recovery team expected almost certain peril from indigenous, tribal inhabitants" —a savage gang of "headhunters," as Moore called them. The missing plane and its crew lay deep in the wilderness, where

Hal Moore prepares for another winter jump, January 1948. *The Hal Moore Collection*

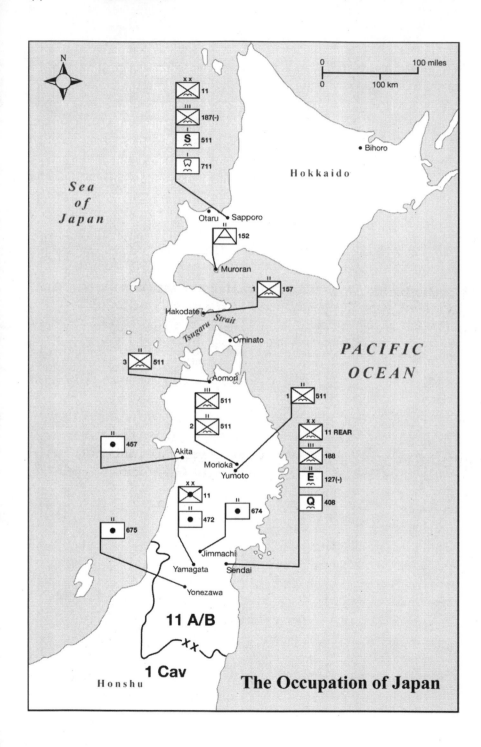

the Indonesian government had little contact with the primitive tribes, and even less interest in governing them. If the Americans wanted to retrieve the remains of their fallen airmen, they would have to do it on their own. And the lost aircrew—assuming any of them had survived the crash—would be fodder for the headhunters unless the Americans got there soon.[33]

Moore and his comrades were briefed in Tokyo, where they rehearsed the mission for several days. However, the morning before their scheduled departure, "the mission was called off because the American government had designated the site of that crash as a US cemetery." Moore never understood why the US had suddenly changed its mind about the rescue, or how they concluded that the airmen were dead, but he tacitly admitted that "we probably would've been killed, jumping into Indonesia and the headhunters."[34]

After two and a half years in Occupied Japan, Moore received orders to the 82nd Airborne Division at Fort Bragg, North Carolina. Departing Camp Crawford with Butch in tow, Hal reported to E Company, 1-505th Parachute Infantry Regiment in June 1948. Once again, he found himself a platoon leader but, as was common throughout the postwar Army, there was very little training being done. As Moore recalled, "most of what we did was escort the remains of dead American soldiers."

The escort detail "was very, very important to me," Hal said, even if it was a little depressing. "There were a lot of World War II dead who had been temporarily buried in Europe and who were now being shipped home for burial close to their families." The bodies arrived stateside in a casket which, in turn, was placed inside a cargo crate. A forklift would load the crate into the baggage car of a train and Moore would have to stay awake all night in the baggage car, sitting on the floor beside the crated body. "If it traveled for two days and two nights," Moore said, "we had to be next to that box every step of the way to make sure that it got home safely to their loved ones." Moore's assignment was to deliver these remains to local morticians across the Southeast—Florida, Georgia, Alabama, and the Carolinas.[35]

Between his train rides, Hal shared the company of a number of beautiful young women, until he won the affections of a particular girl, Julia B. Compton. Born on February 10, 1929 in Fort Sill, Oklahoma, "Julie," as she was known, was the only child of Colonel and Mrs. Louis J. Compton. Hal described her as the "quintessential Army brat"—growing up on several different Army posts during the interwar years. At the height of World War II,

Julie and her mother had lived in Washington DC while her father served overseas in the European Theater. During that time Julie attended and graduated from Chevy Chase Junior College.[36]

Colonel Compton was reassigned to Fort Bragg in 1948, and Julie enrolled at the University of North Carolina, Chapel Hill. "Julie was visiting her parents there [Fort Bragg] in August of that year when the two of us met." Captivated by the nineteen-year-old beauty, Moore recalled that "I burned up the roads between Fayetteville, North Carolina and Chapel Hill during the next year and a half, courting the woman I knew was meant for me."[37]

Returning from one of his weekend excursions to UNC, Moore heard about a unit on the main post "that tested parachutes out of different kinds of airplanes." It developed that the Army Field Forces had set up a detachment known as the Airborne Test Section, whose sole purpose was to test experimental parachutes for the Army, Air Force, and CIA. Commanded by then-Lieutenant Colonel Harry W.O. Kinnard, the unit was aggressively seeking volunteers to test the emerging concept of free-fall parachuting, "not the traditional static line methods," which had been used in World War II.[38]

To this point, recreational skydiving was "just gaining traction" in Europe, and the US Army wanted to test its military applications for higher altitude air insertions. The Air Force, meanwhile, wanted to test these concepts for pilot ejections. The job sounded exciting and certainly more upbeat than looking after a dead soldier's casket on a baggage car. Hal volunteered for the program and made his first jump with the Test Section on November 17, 1948.[39]

Testing parachutes, as Moore found out, certainly was exciting—he nearly lost his life on the first jump. That afternoon, as he exited the aircraft, his parachute got caught on the tail fin. Suddenly, Moore found himself being dragged through the air at over 120 miles per hour, with both pilots unaware that a jumper had been caught on the tail of their plane. As he clung to his shoulder harness, trying to free himself from the entangled chute, fellow paratrooper Sergeant Murray, "was jumping behind me, and as he flew past me, I heard him holler 'Pull!' as in pull my reserve." But Hal Moore knew better. If he pulled his reserve parachute while the plane was travelling in one direction, and the momentum of his reserve chute going in the other direction, his body would have been torn apart by the centrifugal force. Luckily, "the parachute tore free and I was able to activate my reserve."[40]

But this death-defying jump was only the beginning. In July 1949, "I had

Above: The view of Camp Crawford from Moore's Bachelor Officer Quarters during the winter. The harsh Japanese winters gave Moore and his comrades an ideal setting for arctic warfare training. *The Hal Moore Collection*

Left: Hal Moore dons his cross-country ski gear. Every Wednesday and Saturday afternoon, Moore would get off from work early to practice with the Regimental Cross-Country Ski Team. Hal became so adept at the sport that he was offered a chance to compete in the 1948 Olympics. *The Hal Moore Collection*

another malfunction with a free-fall parachute, the XB-14," an Air Force design being tested for high-altitude aircrew evacuations. "I had a total malfunction," Moore said, meaning that his parachute failed to deploy. Jumping from an altitude of only 3,000 feet, the malfunction gave Moore less than five seconds to deploy his reserve chute before he hit the ground. Without a moment's hesitation, Moore activated the reserve, but as soon as he did, the troublesome main chute finally deployed its canopy. With two parachutes deployed, Moore swayed back and forth like a pendulum through the air as he floated to the ground. As a humorous aside, Hal remembered that when he tried to return the parachute's ripcord (an accountable item), the Test Section's supply sergeant let him keep it as a "memento" of surviving the horrific malfunction.[41]

Aside from these hair-raising tales, however, most of Moore's jumps passed without incident. "I never got seriously injured," he said, except "a sprained ankle here and there." In addition to his free fall jumps, Moore also tested a number of parachute life preservers. During his three years with the Airborne Test Section, Moore fondly remembered making over eighty jumps into Pamlico Sound and Tampa Bay.

Left and below: Japanese repatriates returning to Hokkaido from the Empire's former colonies in the Pacific. Moore remembered that repatriating Japanese civilians and POWs was one of the more unpleasant aspects of occupation duty. *The Hal Moore Collection*

The Camp Crawford movie theater, built under Moore's supervision when he became the camp's construction officer. *The Hal Moore Collection*

Japanese children in Wakkanai, 1947. Said Moore of his time in Hokkaido: "I made friends with a lot of the Japanese people." *The Hal Moore Collection*

Right: The Japanese contractors, Hirata and Torchy, provided the technical expertise for Moore's construction projects at Camp Crawford, August 1947. *The Hal Moore Collection*

Below: Fun times with Butch in Sapporo, May 1947. Moore recalled: "I taught that dog how to sit, how to stand, and how to speak." When Hal finally returned to United States in 1948, the dog came with him. *The Hal Moore Collection*

Left: Yamada, the owner of a local Japanese kennel, poses with two German Shepherd pups. During the war, Germany had sent several of these pups to Japan to serve as police dogs in the Kempai Tai. Moore adopted Butch from the litter at Yamada's kennel. *The Hal Moore Collection*

Below: Hal Moore on a leisurely day of hunting. During his downtime, Moore often hunted ducks and other small animals in the Hokkaido countryside. *The Hal Moore Collection*

Moore (far left) and his comrades prepare for a mission to recover the remains of an Air Force utility plane which had crash-landed in the jungles of Indonesia, 1948. However, their mission was cancelled when the US Government decided to leave the plane where it lay. *The Hal Moore Collection*

Splashing down in Tampa Bay, Florida, 1949. While assigned to the Airborne Test Section, Moore jump-tested a variety of experimental parachutes and parachute life preservers for the Army, Air Force, and CIA. *The Hal Moore Collection.*

Right: Moore (left) prepares for a daylight jump with the Airborne Test Section at Fort Bragg, 1949. *The Hal Moore Collection*

Below: Wrangling a parachute after touching down on Sicily Drop Zone at Fort Bragg, North Carolina, 1949. *The Hal Moore Collection*

Meanwhile, Hal and the young Miss Compton fell even more in love with one another. He proposed in the spring of 1949, and the couple set their marriage date for November 22 of that year. The usual wedding announcements went out to the Fayetteville *Observer*, but Moore, with his customary wit, penned the following letter to the paper's lifestyle columnist:

"I'm getting tired of reading about all those weddings where the bride gets all the credit, so I have written this which I would like you to print in your column:

LT. HAROLD G. MOORE GETS MARRIED

On Tuesday morning, 22 November 1949, Main Post Chapel, Lt. H.G. Moore of Kentucky and Fort Bragg, was married by Chaplain (Major) S.W. Kane. The groom was handsomely attired in a forest green blouse of elastique with semi-yoke collar tailored expressly by Brooks Brothers of New York over elastique slacks of the ever popular sunset pink. Both blouse and slacks had been recently pressed. Nonchalantly yet tastefully placed about his blouse were several stunning old gold and silver scatter-pins. On either side of his collar were two pairs of miniature crossed rifles, which signified that Lt. Moore is in the Infantry. This gay [cheerful] touch was complemented by two tiny US's immediately above the rifles denoting that Lt. Moore is a member of the US Army. On either shoulder was a small slightly tarnished silver bar which told all the world that the groom was a Lieutenant. His only ornament which he wore over his heart was a pair of curling silver wings bounding a miniature silver parachute. Lt. Moore was once a member of the 11th Airborne Division and world-famed 82nd Airborne Division. His shirt was of eggshell brown with a rich brown cravat tied with a half-Windsor around a stand-up collar.

For something old, the groom wore a pair of shoes purchased in late 1944 and recently whole-soled. For something new, he wore a snow white undershirt with 1/4 sleeves, a Quartermaster model from the Main Post. For something borrowed, Lt. Moore carried a small rabbit's foot in his watch pocket which he had taken from a close friend on the morning of the wedding in a fit of panic when he realized just how close it was. For something blue, Lt. Moore wore a stunning pair of blue garters bounded with a red fringe. His forest green

Hal and Julie
on their wedding
day, November
23, 1949. *The
Hal Moore
Collection*

hat of fur felt was a flighter model by Bancroft matching his blouse
and was set at a rakish angle upon leaving the church.

Miss J. Compton was also present whom he married. She wore
a dress. Also shoes. Immediately after the ceremony, Lt. Moore retired to the home of Colonel and Mrs. Compton for a much needed
drink of milk with the Father of the Bride. After frantic and unsuccessful attempts to evade numerous well-wishers, Lt. Moore left on
a wedding trip.

On his return, Lt. Moore will pick up his dog from Colonel and
Mrs. Compton, and make his home at Garrilands."[42]

Tickled by his unorthodox humor, the senior editor put Hal Moore's announcement in the next available morning edition. But as Hal and Julie began
their lives as newlyweds, a war was brewing on the Korean Peninsula.

American GIs prepare a howitzer position near the Kum River, July 15, 1950. In the opening stages of the UN intervention, many predicted that Korea would be an easy victory.

US Army photo

CHAPTER THREE

KOREA

orea had been a Japanese colony from its annexation in 1910 until the end of World War II. Following the Allied victory over Japan, the United States and the Soviet Union divided the peninsula into two political zones along the 38th Parallel. The north became a Communist state while the south remained capitalist. However, on June 25, 1950, the North Korean People's Army (NKPA) stormed across the 38th Parallel with the goal of reuniting the peninsula under Communist rule.

The conflict was unique for the US military because it wasn't a "war" in the traditional sense—there had no formal declaration of hostilities and it was the first conflict carried out under the banner of the recently formed United Nations (UN). President Harry Truman therefore dubbed it a "police action." At first glance, however, it appeared that the conflict was a minor adjunct of World War II. The military used much of the same weaponry and tactics as it had during the previous war. At the higher echelons, Korea featured much of the same cast from World War II. General Douglas MacArthur, who had made headlines during the Philippine campaign, returned as commander-in-chief of UN forces. General Omar Bradley was now Chairman of the Joint Chiefs and General J. Lawton Collins, who had headed the VII Corps in Europe, was now the Army Chief of Staff. Lieutenant General Matthew Ridgway, an airborne pioneer and former commander of the 82nd Airborne Division, returned as commander of the Eighth US Army.[43]

Although the invasion had caught the US by surprise, many predicted that Korea would be an easy victory. General MacArthur cheerfully predicted that his troops would be home by Christmas 1950. Others thought that the North Koreans would simply quit the field as soon as they discovered they were fighting Americans. After all, the US had just defeated Germany and Japan—who were the North Koreans to tussle with America's war machine? However, the Army of 1950 was a far cry from the eight-million-man force which had defeated the Nazis and Imperial Japan five years earlier. Training and readiness had sunk to an all-time low after the US demobilized its army and discharged its wartime conscripts. By 1949, a soldier's typical day consisted of little more than constabulary duty, organized athletics, and USO dances. Thus, in the opening stages of the war, the US paid a terrible price for its unpreparedness.

After a disastrous encounter at the Battle of Osan, the atrophied American forces retreated south to the port of Pusan, where they rallied to make their final stand against the NKPA. For six weeks, UN troops (consisting mostly of American, British, and South Korean forces) beat back North Korean assaults in what became known as the Pusan Perimeter—a 140-mile defensive line around the city. After a miraculous break-out from Pusan, and the Allies' amphibious landing at Inchon, the Americans rallied a counter-offensive which pushed the North Koreans back beyond the 38th Parallel all the way to the Yalu River on the country's northern border with China.

Meanwhile, "1950 and 1951 were very rough years for our family," Moore said. In the summer of 1950, his brother Bill contracted polio—a disease which left him crippled from the waist down. At the time, Bill was a junior at the University of Notre Dame and a starting member of the "Fighting Irish" football team. Battling his disease, Bill spent the next several months at the Roosevelt Rehabilitation Center in Warm Springs, Georgia, where Hal and Julie visited him often. Although Bill survived his bout with polio, it left him bound to a pair of leg braces for the remainder of his life. The following June, Moore's father died from a massive heart attack. The death of Harold Sr. devastated the family—especially Mary. "My mother had the strength and love of God to lead our family for the next fifty years, without Dad. She and her God were a great team for the Moore family after Dad's death."[44]

As the war in Korea raged on, Hal remained stateside with the Airborne Test Section at Fort Bragg. Even though the situation looked bleak for the UN forces, Hal wrote to his mother that "I am in no immediate danger of being sent out."

Still, it weighed on heavily on his mind.

He wondered if his first test as a combat leader might come on the battlefields of North Korea. While comforting his mother in the wake of Harold Sr.'s death, Hal was ordered back to Fort Benning to attend the nine-month Infantry Officer's Advanced Course (IOAC). A continuation of the Basic Course, IOAC prepared junior captains for company command and battalion staff.[45]

Before leaving Fort Bragg, Hal and Julie welcomed the birth of their first child, Harold Gregory Moore III, or "Greg" as they called him. Born in May 1951, Greg was a healthy baby boy and was soon followed by a brother, Steven, born in May 1952 at Martin Army Hospital on Fort Benning. But while celebrating his new life as a doting father, Moore finished the Advanced Course with orders to Korea. He was granted a one-month furlough, which he spent with his wife and mother in Bardstown, before deploying to Korea in June 1952. "I boarded a plane in Louisville, Kentucky, and left Julie standing there with two babies in her arms," ages fourteen months and six weeks.[46]

After the breakout from the Pusan Perimeter, UN forces had the North Koreans on their heels and, for a while, it appeared as though a UN victory was inevitable—until the Communist Chinese entered the fight. Throughout the

Moore poses with his infant son, Greg. Born in May 1951, Greg would be followed by four siblings over the next ten years. *The Hal Moore Collection*

The calm before the storm, 1952. Hal and Julie stand with their two sons, newborn Steven (left) and one-year-old Greg (right). Within a few months, Moore would deploy to the battlefields of North Korea. *The Hal Moore Collection*

Feigning fascination with a science fiction novel at Camp Stoneman, California, 1952. Stoneman was a major staging area for US servicemen deploying to the Korean War. *The Hal Moore Collection*

fall of 1950, a huge Chinese counteroffensive regained much of the land which had been lost to UN forces following the Inchon landings. By January 1951, the Communists had reoccupied Seoul and had pushed the UN as far south as Wongju, where the frontlines had stabilized. However, during their blitzkrieg to Seoul, the Chinese had outrun their supply lines, allowing the UN to regain the initiative and roll back the Communist tide through a series of counterattacks including Operation Roundup, Operation Killer, and Operation Ripper—the latter of which expelled the Communists from Seoul.

That spring, the Chinese attempted one more counteroffensive before being halted by the US X Corps in May 1951. By month's end, the Eighth US Army counterattacked and re-established the frontlines just north of the 38th Parallel. For the remaining two years of the war, the UN Command and the Red Chinese continued fighting, but exchanged little ground.

When Moore arrived in Korea in the summer of 1952, the major offenses had ended and the war had devolved into a stalemate. "Peace talks," for what they were worth, had been underway for nearly a year and both American and Communist forces had dug themselves into a network of trenches, each making minor advances against the other in bloody skirmishes across the mountainous terrain.[47]

The first leg of Moore's trip to Korea took him to Camp Stoneman, California. Located at the edge of the San Francisco Bay area, Stoneman had been a major staging area for the US Army during World War II. "This particular part of California is bleak," Hal wrote to his wife, "brown hills, no trees." He

Wake Island, June 1952. Moore stands in front of an old Japanese Type 95 tank, a reminder of the life-and-death struggles of the Pacific War. *The Hal Moore Collection*

described Stoneman as "the usual Repple Depple type but I didn't expect it to be the Vale of Kashmir." Still, Moore was happy to have a hot meal and a hot shower—a remarkable improvement from the replacement depot he had seen in the Philippines.

"Fort Benning loused up on their processing," Moore's letter continued. "In short, I am supposed to have a certain list of clothing—ODs [olive drab fatigues], extra boots, Ike jacket, etc.—in addition to what I have. No one has everything of course. I understand that when I get to Korea, it will be wise to 'travel light' so I am leaving here with very little."[48]

Hal spent most of his time at Stoneman reading books, going to Mass, or enjoying the tame nightlife of the Bay Area—there was little to do on the base. Throughout his first week, several new officers were flown in daily from various parts of the country. On June 19, 1952, he wrote that this influx of new officers probably meant that he would be shipping out soon. "I figure that we will be leaving here this weekend sometime," he said. "I also understand that we are faced with four or five days in Japan followed by a 36-hour train ride to Sasebo [near Nagasaki], then boat to Korea to another Repple Depple for an indeterminate amount of time. Facing it all ahead, I figure I shall get to a unit by late July. This means about six more weeks of lying around waiting. However, that is the life of a replacement. I have tried to develop a certain patient philosophy about these times . . . I try not to dwell too much on the tedious journey ahead. This next 18 months is a necessary evil which must be faced and I know I can do it."[49]

Moore's premonition of the impending departure proved correct—he and the other officers left Camp Stoneman the following weekend. The night before his departure, Hal recalled that "I got to sleep at 3:00 a.m. and was awakened at 9:30 a.m. by an announcement over the squawk-box that the plane group I was in would leave at *9:45 a.m.* So I had 15 minutes to shave, dress, pack, etc. Most everyone was caught in the sack like me. After waiting 11 days; 15 minutes! So I hit the panic button and packed stuff everywhere—I made it to formation at 9:55. So then we all waited for an hour. Apparently for no reason. Then the bus left for Travis AFB where we were told to eat a quick lunch as we'd take off at 1 p.m."[50]

Climbing aboard a Trans Ocean Airline flight—"a chartered civilian plane with plush seats"—Moore departed Travis Air Force Base and landed on Wake Island twenty-two hours later. During their final descent into Wake, the pilot "circled it several times, so we all had a great look at it. What a hot, barren place! No trees—the highest bush is about six feet. I enjoyed rubbernecking at the old bunkers where [Major James] Devereux and his Marines fought. We were loaded into a bus and driven around the perimeter of the island to the mess hall for a hot meal of spare ribs."

Following the short layover on Wake Island, Moore's departing flight to

Mortar company commander, Captain Hal Moore, in the Hantan River Valley. August 8, 1952. *The Hal Moore Collection*

Japan had to make an emergency landing on Iwo Jima due to a typhoon which had settled over Tokyo. "That didn't make me mad," Hal said, "as I was tired and cramped after 31 hours of flight." Spending the night in Iwo Jima was a welcome break. He had been in his final semester at the Academy when the invasion of Iwo Jima began, and now the island was one of the many US enclaves in the Pacific. Grabbing a hot shower and a cold beer, he thought about the hard-won battle which had been fought on this island seven years earlier. "I had a good look at Mt. Suribachi of the flag-raising fame. It was all very quiet and peaceful in the morning—but the rusted AAA [anti-aircraft artillery] and beat-up

Jap equipment gave mute evidence of the hell it was in May of '45."[51]

Taking off at 8:00 a.m. on June 25, Moore's plane landed at Camp Drake in Japan four hours later. His first day at the camp was filled with the normal variety of in-processing and, surprisingly, Hal ran into several of his old friends from the 11th Airborne Division. Although the incoming replacements were being sent to various divisions across the UN battlefront, Hal and many of his fellow airborne veterans received orders to the 7th Infantry Division. As it turned out, the new Commanding General of the 7th Division had also commanded the 11th Airborne and was eager to see his old paratroops in the ranks of his new command.

The day after his arrival, Hal and his fellow replacements were treated to a series of one-hour lectures: one on the history of Korea, one on the UN troop movements, and one on the various health and safety tips needed to survive the Korean climate. "The officers returning from Korea through here strongly advise travelling light," he wrote to Julie. "They have a baggage warehouse set up here where you can leave your Val-Paks packed with the clothes you don't take. They band them and wrap them up in paper."

While settling into Camp Drake, he was surprised to see how much Japan had changed in the past four years—"cleaner and of course the peace treaty

Captain Hal Moore becomes the Operations Officer (S-3) of the 17th Infantry Regiment. In this photograph, the departing S-3, Major Byrl Taylor, hands off his Jeep to the incoming Captain Moore near Chip-ori, Korea– August 13, 1952. The Jeep later became a casualty of war when it sustained a direct hit from an enemy artillery shell during the Battle of Triangle Hill. *The Hal Moore Collection*

brought a lot of changes," he continued in his letter to Julie. The following day, the camp quartermaster issued Hal the first set of field gear which he would need for Korea—"two sets of fatigues, duffel bag, two GI blankets, poncho, mess gear, mosquito net, carbine, ammo pouches," and some extra pairs of fatigues, boots, and socks. With his orders to the 7th Division, Moore boarded his westbound train to Yokohama at 3:15 in the morning and embarked on a troop transport to Pusan later that afternoon. "Very few go by air to Korea," he said. The boat ride, which took him through the straights between Honshu and Kyushu, featured an on-board movie theater and, according to Hal, too much food for what little activity they did.

After two days at sea, Moore arrived in Korea on July 1, 1952.[52]

Hustling through the Eighth Army's Replacement Depot, Moore was assigned to the 17th Infantry Regiment, situated along the UN's Main Line of Resistance (MLR) north of the 38th Parallel. Arriving at the front, however, he was surprised to learn who his enemy really was. For a war which presumably was being fought against North Korea, the only enemy combatants he saw were Chinese. Indeed, by this stage of the war, most of the engagements were between the Americans and Red Chinese.

After less than a week on the frontline, Moore was given command of the regiment's heavy mortar company. Now, as a young Captain, he finally had the opportunity to lead troops in combat. At first, the prospect of taking over a new company in a combat zone—while trying to learn the culture of the regiment—seemed overwhelming. However, in a letter written to Julie on July 6, 1952, he reported that "by now, I have my feet a bit more firm on the ground—it will take about three more weeks, however, until I really get to know all the various SOPs, officers, etc. in the regiment."[53]

Hal looked forward to leading his new troops, but he was less impressed with the company's departing commander. "The fellow who has this company leaves on the 8th [of July]," he wrote. "He will turn the company over to me tomorrow. From what I've seen so far, this is a pretty good bunch of men but there is plenty that needs shaping up. The present company commander is an obscene, loud, rabbit-faced person who is interested only in getting back to the USA. The Colonel had him pegged, though, as he told me that he [the departing commander] had lost interest in the company. Apparently, all that he is interested in is cheating on his wife as he is continually boasting of his affairs in the past, and to come, en route to his home, wife, and children. I

Moore (second from right) stands with the rest of the 17th Infantry Regimental Staff, August 1952. *The Hal Moore Collection*

Colonel Lawrence S. Reynolds, Commander of the 17th Infantry Regiment, November 1952. Reynolds commanded the regiment during the action on Triangle Hill. *The Hal Moore Collection*

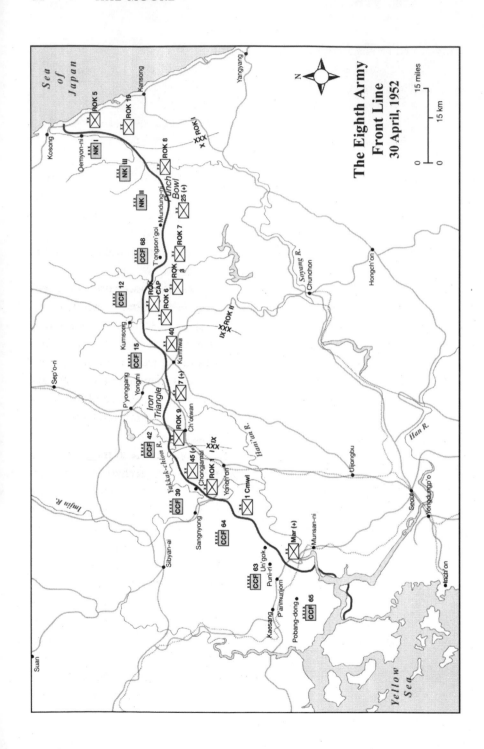

The Eighth Army Front Line 30 April, 1952

can tell that he has no character whatsoever and I can hardly wait for him to leave so that I can shake this company up. There'll be some changes made."

A few days later, Hal had his first taste of combat. Together with his forward observer, he directed some 1,800 mortar rounds onto an enemy-occupied hill. The mission, Moore said, prevented the Chinese from massing reinforcements in the 17th Infantry's area. "Also, we support a lot of patrol activities," Moore wrote. Indeed, Hal's mortarmen were frequently on standby to disperse an enemy ambush or disrupt an enemy attack. "The company CP [command post] where I hang my hat is about 2,800 yards behind the MLR. I spend a lot of my time out with the platoons, though. Life is very good around here. Fine chow and a good, dry place to sleep with cot and all. No complaints whatsoever. I know that my time over here will prove very educating and I certainly hope that I have a variety of jobs."[54]

After a few days with the company, Moore realized what a great group of men he had under his command. It was a shame that their previous commander had been such a toxic leader. "The men have been abused," he wrote. The NCOs had been shunned, the subordinate officers had been alienated, and they were frequently under-fed—"so I have my work cut out for me." Moore immediately made it known that a new command climate was in effect. He broke down the barriers of distrust among his officers and NCOs by seeking their advice on tactical matters; and his men reciprocated by showing their commander the intricacies of mortar and fire support.

"One of my first acts as CO [commanding officer] was to move six men out of the worst 'boar's nest' in the place." These mortarmen had been billeted in a derelict bunker infested with rodents. "I moved them into the officer's bunkers and I moved us down there [into the mortermen's old bunker]. I had some Korean support troops clean it first, though, and it is very adequate for my Gunnery Officer, Recon Officer, Warrant Officer, and myself. A few mice and bugs, but not bad. Also, one corner of my end was dug into an old Korean grave which was immediately covered, but there is a small odor. I keep my feet down at that end, though, and by liberal use of an aerosol bomb and opening the door, it's not bad sleeping at all. These graves are hard to avoid since they are scattered helter-skelter all over these hills where our positions are." He also took the initiative to build showers for the platoons and the company command post. "It beats an hour round-trip on the dusty roads to the regimental shower point," Hal said. "The men are cleaner—and whether they realize it or not, they are near their place of duty and available for fire missions."[55]

Chinese infantrymen resort to throwing rocks at their UN attackers during the Battle of Triangle Hill. Moore recalled being dumbfounded by the enemy's tactics. For instance, the Chinese were notorious for sending their infantry formations through their own artillery screen. This often led to massive incidents of fratricide. *PLA photo.*

By the end of his first week in command, Hal noted that he was "catching on to the theory of this arty [artillery] business slowly . . . I certainly will have a thorough knowledge of fire support—the lack of which very often separates the men from the boys." Eager to put his knowledge to good use, Moore often went out with his forward observers and the combat patrols. He relished these opportunities because he always felt that a commander's place was on the battlefield with his troops—not sitting comfortably at a CP miles away from the front lines.

"Our whole MLR is under direct observation from the enemy," Hal noted after returning from a mortar mission. "However, he [the enemy] does not fire too much—why? No one knows. Every now and then he does. For instance, on 8 June, this CP area took 182 rounds of 122mm arty. Everyone's ok though—these bunkers are *really built.*" Most of the Chinese tactics made little sense to him. For example, the enemy would often attack in waves of personnel without any regard to tactical formations or economy of fire-power.[56]

One month into his new command, Hal was the busiest he had ever been.

As part of the company's leadership change, he had been given two new NCOs—both of whom had combat experience in World War II—and a crop of new lieutenants. "This is a really good job I have," he wrote to Julie. "No boredom of sitting on the Main Line of Resistance looking through a hole in the bunker." Instead, he spent considerable time moving along the regimental front coordinating mortar fire among the battalions.

Speaking with the frontline commanders, "I felt that I had my feet on the ground well enough to make a few recommendations on better support for the actions we've been in." By mid-July 1952, the regiment's actions had been confined to taking prisoners and conducting small-scale raids. "So I could see no reason why three platoons of mortars should remain behind the MLR where they could not render close support to these [new] patrols."

Thus, by coordinating with the adjacent regiments, Moore would move either one or two patrols to the Outpost Line of Resistance every night. He would discuss the fire support plan with the patrol leaders the day before the mission and let them make adjustments based on where they felt they needed the heaviest mortar concentration. If a patrol got lost, Moore would fire White Phosphorous rounds against certain landmarks so the patrol could trace its way back to friendly lines. "It's really working out fine," Hal wrote. "I have walked patrols back which couldn't possibly have executed a proper withdrawal because of carrying wounded and equipment. On three separate mornings recently, both Battalion Commanders on the line and the Regimental Commander have complemented the mortar company at the morning briefing—so I feel like I am helping the effort somewhat."

Apparently, the Regimental Commander liked Moore's handling of the mortarmen so much that he invited him to be the Regimental Operations Officer (S-3). A billet typically occupied by a Major, an S-3 was responsible for planning maneuvers and training operations. Many officers who had successful tenures as a Battalion or Regimental S-3 went on to achieve higher rank. It was an awesome responsibility for a young Captain, but Moore remained confident that he could handle the job. "The only thing is, I must become familiar with about thirty different offensive, defensive, and counterattack [options] in addition to the current operation handling."[57]

On his last night with the mortar company, Hal recalled a vicious firefight between an American patrol and an enemy ambush. "I had a platoon well forward of the Outpost Line of Resistance to support a long-range patrol. The patrol ran into a Chinese ambush, was surrounded, and had quite a fight.

Those four tubes fired all night from 2130 [9:30 p.m.] to 0945 using 845 High Explosive and 755 White Phosphorous. It prevented the Chinese from reinforcing, and covered the patrol's withdrawal. The mortar position took 79 incoming—one right through the FDC bunker—no one wounded and nothing went out of action. I was awful proud of these men as I know they had a lot to do with preventing that patrol from really being cut up. So I left the company with a good action."

While Moore settled into his new job as the Regimental S-3, Colonel Richard Risden turned over his command of the regiment to Colonel Lawrence S. Reynolds, who had just completed his tour as the Division Chief of Staff. Under Reynolds' command, Hal said that "we were jumping through ourselves in an intense training program." Within only a few weeks, Moore had drafted three anti-airborne operations, three minor penetration plans, three regimental attacks, and made a complete reconnaissance of the 7th Division's sector. Taken together, these tasks gave Hal Moore a recurring 17-hour workday.

This intense planning, however, would soon prove to be beneficial, for by mid-September Chinese incursions were back on the rise. In a letter dated September 17, 1952, Hal wrote, "I think we'll be on the line here for quite some time now. At present, we're strengthening our positions. The Chinese are looking right down our throats. His high ground includes Hills 717 and 1062 [near the infamous Triangle Hill]. Our Main Line of Resistance is strictly on ground of the enemy's choosing. He didn't leave us much to work with, but still we have made it into a very strong line."[58]

In September 1952, General James Van Fleet—who had replaced Matthew Ridgeway as the Eighth Army Commander when the latter assumed command of UN Forces—submitted the offensive plans for Operation Showdown, a low-level attack designed to push the Chinese defensive line 1,250 yards farther north. The decisive point of the attack focused on a ridgeline two kilometers wide near Kimwha. Dominated by three massive hills, this forested ridge was collectively known as the Triangle Hill Complex. However, amidst the ongoing peace conference at Panmunjom, Operation Showdown remained on the backburner.

By October 1, however, the peace negotiations had stalled. The most contentious issue for the negotiating parties was the repatriation of Chinese and North Korean POWs. Unsurprisingly, a number of Communist POWs begged for political asylum in South Korea and Taiwan. Nevertheless, China and North Korea demanded that the soldiers be repatriated to their countries of origin, regardless of personal preference. Feeling that the negotiations were doomed to fail, the Chinese decided to hedge their bets and began launching preparatory strikes from the Iron Triangle on October 3. "That night, we took about 600 rounds of mixed mortar and artillery in our sector," Hal recalled. The attack left two Americans killed and seven wounded.[59]

Three days later, the Chinese intensified their attack. "I don't think I'll ever forget that period from 6–20 October when the Chinese began their limited objective attacks and we retaliated with the Triangle Hill action. At about 1815 on the 6th, we were having our pre-dinner drinks—I was on my second—and the phone call came that our entire 1st Battalion Main Line of Resistance was under attack and that our outposts were being overrun—just then, the rounds started crumpling in the Regimental Command Post. I grabbed a piece of cheese and a cracker and that was my last meal for two and a half days. That, combined with no sleep, was a great deal." Meanwhile, negotiations at Panmunjom failed on October 8, 1952 and Operation Showdown went forward. The Battle of Triangle Hill had begun.

In his next letter home, dated October 18, he described his actions against enemy over the previous two weeks:

Standing guard at the UN POW Camp in Koje-Do, January 1953. The Koje-Do camp held nearly 40,000 Chinese and North Korean POWs. *The Hal Moore Collection*

Hal Moore receives the Army Commendation Medal for his work as the Regimental Operations Officers. February, 1953. *The Hal Moore Collection*

We had two outposts hit—they were platoon-size—the Chinese threw in a terrific barrage of artillery and mortars, all on the button. Then they followed up with an assault right through it.

Moore could hardly believe his eyes—throughout the battle, the Chinese sent waves of infantrymen through their own artillery screen. From a tactical standpoint, it was a senseless move which killed many of their own men before they even reached the American lines. The few Chinamen who did make it through the artillery screen did so with such an unflinching precision that Moore thought they must have been under the influence of drugs. "They take a lot of casualties, but don't seem to care. We've killed 200 in three days—I've counted. And we've taken over 20,000 rounds [of mortar and artillery] in the regimental sector."[60]

Moore's letter continued, "There's been a heck of fight in the ROK's sector to our left. I have a liaison officer over there and he says that the Chinese have had over 2,200 slaughtered. As I write this I can still hear the guns and shellbursts. Their small arms don't hurt us much, but their artillery and mortar fire is brutal and they know how to use it." Indeed they did—on the first night of their attack, Moore's Jeep took a direct hit from a 76mm shell. Fortunately, he wasn't in the vehicle at the time, but it was another three weeks before he received a new Jeep.

In his next letter describing the action on Triangle Hill, Moore wrote:

Division G2 estimates that these Chinese attacks will continue with the intent being to whittle down our people. They will do that, of course, but in the meantime will be cut to pieces—provided we can get our men to dig deep and come up fighting when the barrage slackens.

We had a successful raid on a hill called Sugarloaf—only three friendly WIA; killed about twenty Chinese. Then, the General ordered us to take back an outpost position he had previously agreed we should withdraw from because of its lack of cover and difficulty of resupply. We hit it with a company and they took it, but the Chinese resorted to their old tactics of counterattacking through their own artillery and mortar preparation. We had to pull off—forty WIA and two killed. I think the Chinese kill as many of their own as we do with artillery.

A ROK outpost two miles forward of the ROK unit on our left fell early one evening and we had to counterattack out of the division sector, per the General's order, with a company of our reserve battalion. It was pitch dark and they had never been in the sector before. Their route to the outpost was forward of the Main Line of Resistance through AP [anti-personnel] minefields and were led by a ROK guide who got the company lost four times. Their mission was to restore the outpost and rescue an American artillery FO [forward observer] and reconnaissance sergeant who were still alive on it and calling down artillery on the position for three hours after it had been overrun. That night, a ROK company relieved our people on the hill and they've been fighting for it ever since.

The mission of these Chinese local attacks is to cause casualties so as to better their position at Panmunjom and the UN Assembly. Knowing that, I don't understand why the General wanted to go through with it—especially since the hill is out forward of the Main Line of Resistance and at the base of a Chinese-held mountain. The news calls it Triangle Hill.

All three battalions of the 31st [another regiment fighting in the Triangle Hill area] were decimated ... their 2nd Battalion was down to 200 men. So then, the General began committing other battalions of the Division—first the 32nd's reserve battalion, and it was cut up.

Two nights ago at 0400, I had a call from the G-3 [Division Operations Officer] to get our reserve battalion on trucks and over to the 32nd. They arrived at 1000 and counterattacked [while] elements of the 17th, 31st, and 32nd were fighting on the hill. The hill and environs are now being held by the 2nd and 3rd Battalions of the 17th under the command of the 32nd [Regiment]. Assorted heavy mortars of all three regiments and a hodge-podge of medics and other service elements are all tangled up supporting it. I expect a heavy Chinese counterattack tonight and subsequent commitment of our 1st Battalion. In expectation of that, I have had the officers of the battalion do a recon of the scene of the action. I've never seen such a mess. I think the only way it can be straightened out is for the whole Division to go into reserve and everyone gravitate back to where he belongs.[61]

By October 21, however, most of the action had died down. Throughout the preceding week, the Chinese had suffered some 4,000 casualties. This catastrophic loss of manpower left them with only one division to combat the UN forces on Triangle Hill. Nevertheless, the Chinese refused to quit. "We had our 2nd and 3rd Battalions on Triangle Hill," Moore said, "and a Chinese regiment counterattacked." During the engagement, 3rd Battalion had every officer in all three of its rifle companies wounded or killed; and each company was cut down to less than 100 men before being relieved by a battalion from the 32nd Regiment.[62]

However, on October 25, General Van Fleet pulled the 7th Division off Triangle Hill and turned the area over to the ROK 2nd Division. The battle continued for another month but, in the face of mounting UN casualties, Van Fleet halted the ROK attack on November 28. Triangle Hill would go down in history as the bloodiest battle of 1952.

When the 7th Division rotated off the line, Hal's regiment moved the island of Koje where they were put in charge of a POW Camp, guarding some 45,000 North Korean and Chinese Communists. "In the midst of it all," Moore said,

Colonel William Hardick, 17th Infantry Regimental Commander during the Battle of Pork Chop Hill. *The Hal Moore Collection*

"we had a new Colonel shipped in to us as a replacement for Colonel Reynolds—Colonel William L. Hardick. The Regimental Staff lives in a nice Quonset on the bayside. The MP group that's here extended the courtesies of their very lush Officers' Club one-half mile away. I feel that we will be here until late January [1953]. I hope it's not longer as already I am impatient to get back on the line. However, we aren't losing men here and that helps."

During his time at Koje, Hal served as the assistant commandant of the POW camp. "This is quite unique duty down here," he wrote. "Every now and then, these birds act up. Like one day last week, a group of them pounced on an unarmed work supervisor and beat him up. Needless to say, they were severely disciplined. I have my own private belief, however, that this POW camp is a powder keg." Privately, Moore feared that if the enemy launched another offensive on the mainland, it would precipitate a mass breakout, or a prison riot, at the Koje camp. No such riot ever came, but Moore nonetheless prepared for one. "I have my plans made and disseminated," he wrote. "If they try anything while we're here, they won't get far."[63]

In fact, Moore had devised a unique way of punishing the troublemakers within his camp. Whenever the prisoners misbehaved, he removed the toilet paper from their latrines. "The Chinese were really, really tough soldiers . . . and they had probably been wiping their backsides with leaves and sticks since their supply system undoubtedly prioritized bullets over creature comforts." In the POW camp, however, they had grown accustomed to things like toilet paper and indoor plumbing. Thus whenever Moore removed the toilet paper, it normally took one day (i.e. the course of a few bowel movements) before things quieted down.[64]

By Christmas, Moore learned that he and his comrades were rotating back onto the line. This time, however, they would occupy the area surrounding T-Bone, Old Baldy, and Pork Chop Hill. Returning to his duties as the S-3, Moore flew with Colonel Hardick back to the peninsula for a fast trip across the 7th Division's MLR. Looking at the terrain and the regiment's proposed sector, Hal was soon back to work drafting the various counterattack and defense plans.

The regiment's first stop en route to the frontline was Sindam-ni, nearly fifty miles south of the UN lines. On January 17, 1953, Hal reported that "most of

A photograph taken by Moore from the K Company Sector looking north into the enemy territory. As a rifle company commander, Moore frequently traded fire with the Communist Chinese.
The Hal Moore Collection

the regiment has closed here now and begins training tomorrow." After their low-intensity mission of guarding enemy POWs, it was time for the 17th Infantry to resharpen its fighting skills. "I also have gotten most of the key personnel through a ground reconnaissance in case we are committed in a counterattack." The following week, Moore's regiment moved into the T-Bone Hill sector, where they relieved the battle-weary 31st Infantry.[65]

In the midst of occupying their sector, however, a firefight broke out on the southern slope of T-Bone. "Troops of the 31st actually conducted a three-platoon attack supported by air and armor." According to Moore, their mission was merely to "capture a prisoner"—a dubious objective considering that the platoons took nearly seventy casualties in the process. Moore observed the operation from atop a nearby outpost and, in the middle of the fight, the regiment's personnel carriers—which had been evacuating the wounded—became stranded on one side of a creek where a fording site had been rendered impassable. "I went out there to see what I could do to help," he said. Arriving on the scene, Moore established a shuttle point which carried the wounded GIs around a bypass for the next few hours.

After that treacherous first day on T-Bone Hill, Moore spent most of January refining his battle plans for the regiment. Around this time, he also learned that he had been recommended for an early promotion to Major. Apparently, his performance on the Regimental Staff had inspired Colonel Hardick to make the recommendation. Before Hal could pin on his new rank, however, an unexpected twist of fate put him in command of a rifle company.

"This goes back to early December," he said, "when General Smith [the division commander] put a policy, all his own, within the 7th Division that no infantry officers recommended for promotion would be forwarded until they had commanded a rifle platoon or company in combat." Moore had commanded a rifle platoon, but it had been with the Army of Occupation in Hokkaido—and according to the General's new policy, Moore's previous command of the mortar company held no weight. Thus, Hal could not be promoted until he had commanded a rifle company on the frontline.[66]

Nevertheless, the Division Commander knew what his policy meant for the young Captain Moore. "In fact, he dropped in to the Regimental CP in his chopper—specifically to see me—got me off to one side, and told me to tell Colonel Hardick to forward my promotion papers. He would send them [the promotion papers] along and send me down to command a rifle company. He then told me that I had done a fine job as the Heavy Mortar CO and as S-3, and that my services had been requested at Division." As it turned out, General Smith wanted to make Moore his Assistant Division G-3.

In his next letter home, Hal wrote that he was "feeling pretty good about the whole turn of events—so long as the rifle company doesn't appear on any record, as it will look like I fouled up as S-3. I have really learned a lot as the S-3 . . . and will pick up more as the rifle company commander, then up to Assistant G-3 where I'll get a little larger picture. I know I will enjoy commanding a unit again . . . probably get more sleep than I'm getting now."[67]

Hal Moore assumed command of K Company (3rd Battalion, 17th Infantry) on February 4, 1953. Just as he had done with the mortar company, Hal realized that he had inherited a unit which suffered from poor leadership. The previous commander, he noticed, was remarkably similar to the one he had replaced earlier. "This company is sadly lacking in discipline . . . the men are unnecessarily dirty," he wrote. "I am in the process of shaping up a few platoon leaders, including two 2nd Lieutenants of the [West Point] Class of '51." Even though he had inherited another jaded company, Moore relished the opportunity. He later admitted that, "if given the opportunity to take a good unit or a bad unit, I'll take the bad unit every time. With the right motivation and leadership, they have nowhere to go but up."[68]

K Company covered nearly half of the battalion's Main Line of Resistance. To accommodate this large defensive area, the battalion augmented Moore's company with a platoon from nearby L Company, as well as a tank platoon and a section of anti-aircraft artillery. "I am defending a critical sector," he wrote to Julie, "and I think we're fairly well disposed. I am making a few changes, though. The company itself is falling out hard and I am cracking the whip on my platoon leaders. I love command duty anyway and nothing pleases me more than to shape up a unit."

Halfway through Moore's letter, a firefight broke out near the western edge of K Company's defensive line. "I hear the Chinese burp guns [a nickname given to the Soviet-made PPSh-41 machine gun] sputtering off to my left along with some incoming *currumps* [GI slang for the sound of an 81mm mortar]. Some patrol's in a fight. I have my cooks, drivers, typists—'clerks and jerks'—all formed up as a local reserve as all my platoons are on line. I keep a loaded grease gun [M-3 submachine gun] hanging right on my rack along with three magazines of ammo. I can be out of here and moving within five minutes if any of my people get hit."[69]

Throughout his first week in command, K Company saw plenty of action along the regimental front. Late on the night of February 11, one of Moore's listening posts (LP) reported hearing voices and other muffled sounds a few hundred meters in front of them. Moore responded by launching some sixty mortar flares to illuminate their position—a move which revealed eight Chinese soldiers wandering in the open. Startled by the sudden illumination, the wayward Chinamen quickly darted back toward their friendly lines. The LP called in a second round of mortars on the retreating Communists and, soon thereafter, Moore sent a rifle squad to investigate the area. Unfortunately, after two hours, the patrol returned with nothing to report. If the Chinese had taken any casualties, they must have carried them away.

The following night—Moore's thirty-first birthday—he sent an ambush patrol toward the base of an enemy-occupied hill. This twelve-man patrol was part of an elaborate scheme to lure the Chinese out of their bunkers. Earlier, Moore had scheduled an L-19 liaison plane to fly over the enemy front and push out a life-sized dummy rigged with a parachute. During this diversionary flight, Moore's patrol established its position near the site of the parachute landing. Moore hoped that the Chinese would be fooled by the dummy landing and—thinking it was a real paratrooper—send out a patrol to capture it. Unfortunately, "the dummy drop didn't suck out any Chinamen," he said. "That darn thing dropped on a Chinese hill and they still didn't come out. My patrol was set up around it in fifteen minutes. I left them lying around it for three hours, then pulled them halfway back . . . and fired 105 illuminating rounds and visually screened the area with negative results. So I had them come back in. It was a good try."[70]

After less than one month in command, Moore was recalled to Division Headquarters to fulfill his role as the Assistant Division G-3. "I guess he [General Smith] considers me purified with a rifle company now," Moore later wrote. "During my time with K Company, I lost more men from enemy shelling than the entire battalion did in six weeks of patrol actions. The principal reason was that I defended a critical flank and had some tanks and AAA on my Main Line of Resistance. As a result, we were the recipients of Chinese harassing, interdictory, and destruction fire all day long—varying in intensity from day to day."[71]

The G-3 position gave him a bird's eye view of all the regiments stationed on the 7th Division front. He enjoyed getting the experience at Division level but, within a week, he admitted that "I am a bit bored back here in this job. I

Moore as the K
Company Com-
mander near
T-Bone Hill,
February 1953.
*The Hal Moore
Collection*

know it's a good experience and a fine opportunity and all, but I miss the
regiment and things that I can directly influence. Everything here is paperwork—no sweat on any of it, I just hate it." Indeed, because of the paperwork,
Hal averaged about five hours of sleep per night. "However, I do have sense
enough to realize that it's an advancement and will help me a lot. I am also
learning a lot about Division and Staff procedure, plus utilization of the
Division Special Troops. Certainly not time lost, but nothing exciting."

Still, life at Division Headquarters was certainly lush by wartime standards. The Staff Officer Mess had a full-service bar where one could buy
martinis, Manhattans, and other fine spirits. Every night after dinner, the officers could see the latest Hollywood films at the division's movie house.[72]

By mid-March, Hal was making regular trips to the frontline to assess
the situation on the ground and relay reports to Division Headquarters. During one of these trips, the Chinese suddenly renewed their offensive along
the 7th Division front. This time, the action focused on Hill 266—the dom-
inant terrain feature in a craggy area known as "Old Baldy." Nearly twelve
miles northeast of Panmunjom, Old Baldy had been the site of four previous
battles between the UN and Communist Chinese. The first battle, in June
1952, ended in a UN victory when defenders from the 45th Infantry Division
halted the Chinese advance. The enemy tried to re-take the hill in July when

the 2nd Infantry Division rotated onto the line. The enemy's July offensive succeeded in taking some ground from the Americans, but the onset of the rainy season stalled their advance. During this lull, the Americans regained the initiative and, by early August, the Chinese had been driven back once again. Undaunted, the enemy tried to seize Old Baldy again in October 1952. After the fourth unsuccessful attempt, the Communists launched their final bid for the hill in March 1953.

From March 23–26, 1953, Moore was caught on the frontline as the Chinese directed their assault on Hill 266. "The Chinese hit our two line regiments—the 17th and the 31st—on the night of the 23rd," he said. "The 17th slaughtered them, but the 31st lost Old Baldy. A counterattack the next day failed to dislodge the Chinese." As part of the UN contingent, a Colombian infantry battalion had been attached to the 7th Division. Throughout the battle, however, Moore noticed that the Colombians were taking the brunt of the enemy's assault. It was a ferocious battle, he said, "reminiscent of Triangle Hill." The Colombians had performed remarkably in the opening stages, but by the afternoon of March 24, they had begun to falter under the Chinese onslaught.[73]

7th Division command post complex, April 1953. Following his command of K Company, Moore became the Assistant Plans and Operations Officer for the Division (Assistant G-3).
The Hal Moore Collection

While Moore was watching the battle from atop a nearby hill, he spied a group of four soldiers crawling and limping away from the south side of Old Baldy. Recognizing them as Colombians, Moore grabbed three nearby soldiers, hopped into his Jeep and quickly descended down the hill. "The four Colombians were wounded, one of them badly," he said. "They were prisoners and the airstrikes had scattered their guards." During the ensuing chaos, they had escaped and were trying to make their way back toward friendly lines. Without a moment's hesitation, Moore tossed the wounded Colombians into the back of his Jeep and drove them to the nearest aid station. For his actions that day, Hal Moore was awarded the Bronze Star.[74]

The following day, however, Moore nearly lost his own life. During a firefight that morning, he and another solider took cover behind a revetment. As they looked over the top of the barricade to assess the enemy situation, the other soldier promptly took a bullet to the head. Moore cringed and yelped in terror as the young soldier fell dead at his feet. "I tried not to think about it. You have to keep your head clear and just let the chips fall where they may." Moore was devastated by the sudden demise of his comrade, but he had to keep his "head in the fight" if he wanted to survive.

Barely a few moments later, a Chinese 81mm mortar landed only fifteen feet away from where Moore was standing. Typically, a mortar would have killed anyone standing that close. The shock wave catapulted Moore head over heels and, when he regained consciousness a few seconds later, he realized that he had been thrown approximately thirty feet. Although it left him with a bad concussion, he had otherwise survived the attack without a scratch. After the battle, he maintained that only the grace of God had saved him.

"We could have taken back that bloody hill if the General had let us counterattack when we wanted to," Moore later wrote. But Division withdrew its forces from Old Baldy, conceding the hill to the Red Chinese.[75]

April 1953 marked the beginning of yet another Chinese offensive. A few miles from Old Baldy was Hill 255—the infamous Pork Chop Hill—a barren and bunkered piece of land which had been part of the 7th Division's front since December 1952. During the final battle for Old Baldy, a Chinese infantry regiment had begun probing the northern slopes of Pork Chop Hill. Satisfied by its apparent vulnerability, the Chinese launched a surprise attack against the American outposts there on April 16, 1953.

Shocked by this sudden incursion, the 31st Infantry sent two of its rifle companies, K and L, to retake the hill. Sadly, both companies had to withdraw after sustaining nearly fifty percent casualties. G Company, from the neighboring 17th Infantry came in as reinforcement, but it too suffered heavy losses. Over the next two days, Companies A, E, and F, from the 17th Infantry led a renewed assault under the cover of artillery fire. Forty-eight hours and 77,000 artillery rounds later, the 17th Infantry had taken back Pork Chop Hill.

Meanwhile, Moore continued pouring over the mountains of paperwork coming into the G-3. In the midst of writing the Division's After-Action Report for Old Baldy, he began soliciting a new assignment—by April 1953, he had approximately three months remaining on his tour and wanted a stateside post where he could decompress after his year in combat. That month, he penned a letter to Brigadier General John H. Michaelis—the Commandant of Cadets at West Point—requesting duty as an instructor in the Department of Tactics. Almost simultaneously, he wrote to Julie telling her that a West Point assignment offered the best of Army glamour—stable hours, regular routines, vast recreational opportunities, and easy access to New York City. After a year of raising their two sons without her husband, it didn't take much to sell Julie on the benefits of an Academy posting.[76]

Back on the frontlines, the 7th Division rebuilt its defenses on Pork Chop Hill. The final negotiations for an armistice were underway at Panmunjom and—from May to June—the skirmishes along Main Line of Resistance had died down. However, on the night of July 6, 1953, the Chinese made their final bid for Pork Chop Hill. Over the next four days, the UN and Chinese-led forces traded fire in an intense battle for control of the hill. Yet just when it seemed that the Americans had the upper hand, the US I Corps commander, Lieutenant General Bruce C. Clarke, decided to abandon Pork Chop Hill on July 11. Two days later, the Chinese reoccupied it.[77]

Both sides suffered heavy losses during the second Battle of Pork Chop Hill. More than 243 US troops were killed in action; 163 were never recovered. Although the US had achieved a 6:1 kill-loss ratio, their objective had been forfeited to the enemy. "I was against it," Moore later wrote. "I felt that we should retake [Pork Chop Hill] but I am not the Division or Corps commander. I have learned over here that you *never* give up ground. You always lose more men in the long run."

Less than three weeks after the Battle of Pork Chop Hill, the negotiating parties at Panmunjom finally reached an accord. The resulting armistice—signed on July 27, 1953—restored the international boundary at the 38th Parallel and established the Korean Demilitarized Zone (DMZ). After the

The 7th Division G-3 Bunker—Moore's "office" for the remainder of the war. April 1953.
The Hal Moore Collection

demarcation agreement, the US kept a permanent military presence along the DMZ to deter any further aggression.

Moore left Korea with a firm conviction that the US had sabotaged its own success. Although the Americans had claimed victory, they had essentially only fought the Communists to a draw. The enemy had dictated the tempo for most of the war and, according to Hal, the Army's rules of engagement discouraged initiative rather than promoted it. For instance, a company commander's actions on the frontline frequently had to get approval from as high as division-level. Moore described it as a "half-garrison, half-combat war" and he often found himself wondering what his objectives were. There seemed to be no reason why the UN forces would suddenly seize a hill, boast about "pushing back" the Chinese defenses, and then suddenly abandon the hill with virtually no explanation. Furthermore, it seemed that the political and higher-echelon leadership didn't have the same desire for "absolute victory" that they had in World War II. Yet Hal remained optimistic that America's next conflict—wherever it may be—would at least be fought on better terms.

CHAPTER FOUR

THE ROAD TO VIETNAM

R eturning to the United States, Moore accepted a new position as an Infantry Tactics Instructor at his revered *alma mater*. After fourteen months in combat, Hal and Julie were glad to settle into a more stabilized assignment. Hal enjoyed working with the cadets, and he took great strides to impart to them his lessons learned in combat. Coincidentally, one of Moore's cadets was a young H. Norman Schwarzkopf, who later went on to command UN forces during the Persian Gulf War. "And I take credit for every one of his accomplishments," Moore said with a facetious grin. Years later, "Stormin' Norman" cited Moore as one of his personal heroes and said that Moore was the reason he chose to branch Infantry.[78]

One of Moore's fellow faculty members, Jim Elkey, recalled, "I was the Executive Officer of the Field Artillery Section . . . where I planned and instructed the cadets in Field Artillery tactics and techniques. My classmate, Hal Moore, was the Executive Officer of the Infantry Section at the same time; and between us we developed a method of showing the cadets how closely the Infantry and Artillery worked together as a team. Hal would have me participate in his Infantry tactics classes in an

Hal and his newborn daughter Julie at West Point, 1955. *The Hal Moore Collection*

85

The Moores' home on the left side of the duplex on the campus of the US Military Academy at West Point, 1954. *The Hal Moore Collection*

appropriate Field Artillery position (Forward Observer, Liaison Officer, etc). During these classes, I tried my best to 'one-up' Hal. Sometimes I succeeded, but in the end he was one step ahead of me."[79]

During his tour at the Academy, Hal and Julie welcomed the birth of their first daughter—also named Julie—in November 1954. Around this time, Moore also began to take notice of the events happening in Indochina. The entire region had been a French colony from 1887 until the rise of the Viet Minh Independence Movement led by Ho Chi Minh in the 1940s. During World War II, Ho Chi Minh had rescued several downed American pilots in Indochina and supplied the US with intelligence on Japanese and Vichy French troop movements. All this, he had hoped, would curry favor with the US government and generate sympathy for the anti-French rebellion. However, Ho Chi Minh had miscalculated America's support for the French and their growing mistrust of all things Communist.

Casting their lot with the French, America responded by sending the Military Assistance Advisory Group (MAAG) to Vietnam in 1950. MAAG was the command group responsible for all US military advisors in foreign countries. Their mission in Vietnam was to supervise the millions of dollars in US equipment being used by the French. By 1953, however, it was clear that the French were losing ground to the Viet Minh.

"We had no TV in those days," Moore said, "we didn't have the money to buy one—and I listened to the radio every night, to the announcers telling about the Battle of Dien Bien Phu. And I grieved over those Frenchmen and their Vietnamese allies because I knew that they were in a difficult position,

The beleaguered French troops take cover in a trench network near Dien Bien Phu, 1954. Their loss to the hands of the Viet Minh at Dien Bien Phu marked the end of French colonial rule in Indochina. *US Army photo*

that they were totally surrounded, that they were going to be defeated." It reminded him eerily of his time in Korea. Just as the Communist Chinese had done, the North Vietnamese were digging trenches and tunnels ever closer to the French positions. Although the Americans had prevailed in Korea, the French had no such luck at Dien Bien Phu. "My wife Julie couldn't understand my fascination with so distant a foreign battle, and I couldn't explain it to her." Yet somehow Moore felt compelled to study the battle and the comparative tactics which led to the French defeat.[80]

Leaving West Point in 1956, Moore attended the Command and General Staff College (CGSC) at Fort Leavenworth for a yearlong course of study. Renowned as one of the toughest schools in the Army, CGSC prepared young majors for the organizational dynamics of Division and Corps-level staff. Moore then reported to the Air Mobility Division in the Office of the Chief of Research and Development at the Pentagon.

"I was a one-man airborne branch and the only man on jump pay." Moore's primary duty was developing new airborne equipment and synchronizing Army-Air Force requirements for airborne operations. "Workweeks were long: 55–65 hours, but exciting." At the Pentagon, "the pressure and stress levels were very high due to the volume of work, long hours, and tight deadlines for decisions involving a lot of money and vast numbers of people. To help control that stress and stay in shape for field duty, every day during lunch hour I either went to the Pentagon Athletic Club and got a workout playing handball or, on alternate days, ran the two miles over to the Lincoln Memorial and back. I'm a firm believer that physical fitness aids mental fitness. My wife got used to me coming home after a tough day and telling her I was so tired I was going out for a run. It always refreshed me and cleared my mind to deal with the two briefcases of work I brought home with me." During these tiresome days at the Pentagon, however, Julie gave birth to their second daughter (and fourth child), Cecile, in December 1958.[81]

"These were also the days of development of the Air Mobility/Air Assault concept," said Moore. In the summer of 1957, Hal's boss, Lt. General James A. Gavin (who had commanded the 82nd Airborne Division during World War II), wrote an article for *Harper's* magazine titled "Cavalry—And I Don't Mean Horses." As the head of Army Research and Development, Gavin envisioned a new method of fighting based on the helicopter. "Jim Gavin's dream was that someday bigger, faster, and better helicopters would carry the infantry into battle. The helicopter, Gavin believed, held the possibility of making the battlefield truly a three-dimensional nightmare for the enemy commander."[82]

Gavin's concept, airmobile infantry, was an extension of the World War II-era doctrine known as "vertical envelopment." Historically, paratroopers and glider-borne infantry had been the only means for achieving vertical envelopment. However, by the late 1950s, Gavin and his colleagues (who included General Hamilton Howze—the Chief of Army Aviation—and Colonel Harry WO Kinnard) were convinced that the helicopter could get better results. However, a strong tide of bureaucratic resentment within the Pentagon would put the airmobile concept on the back-burner for the next few years.[83]

Vo Nguyen Giap (left) and Ho Chi Minh (right) were perhaps the two most prominent figures in the Viet Minh and, later, in North Vietnam's regime. Ho Chi Minh became the president of North Vietnam, while Giap became the supreme commander of the People's Army of Vietnam. *AP Photo*

Moore (far right), his classmates, and their wives, gather for their Ten Year Reunion at West Point, summer 1955. Julie is seated in the front row, second from the right. *The Hal Moore Collection*

Hal Moore receives an oak leaf cluster to his Bronze Star from Colonel Roy J. Herte, Commanding Officer of the 1802nd Special Regiment, West Point's garrison unit. His first Bronze Star had been awarded for rescuing two Colombian soldiers at Old Baldy. The second Bronze Star, as denoted by the oak leaf cluster, was awarded for meritorious service as the Regimental S-3. *The Hal Moore Collection*

Moore (center) inspects the troops during a "Pass and Review" on the Plain at West Point, 1955. *The Hal Moore Collection*

Receiving a championship handball trophy for singles in the Fort Belvoir Handball Tournament from Colonel Ray Adams, the Chief of Staff of the US Army Engineer Center and Fort Belvoir. February 7, 1958. During his time in the Office of the Chief of Research and Development, Moore spent much of his leisure time playing handball, a tradtion he continued when he returned to the Pentagon years later as staff officer and the Deputy Chief of Staff for Personnel. *The Hal Moore Collection*

Ngo Dinh Diem meets with President Eisenhower, 1957. Diem was the first President of South Vietnam and a strong US ally until he was disposed and murdered in a 1963 coup. *National Archives and Records Administration*

Moore poses with his Naval classmates at the Armed Forces Staff College in Norfolk, Virgina, 1960. *The Hal Moore Collection*

Preparing to test a new life preserver over the "dunk tank," Norfolk, Virginia, 1960. *The Hal Moore Collection*

Following graduation from the Armed Forces Staff College in 1960, Moore—now a Lieutenant Colonel—moved his family to Oslo, Norway for his new assignment as a NATO Plans Officer with Allied Forces–Northern Europe. Working with a host of Allied officers, Moore drafted the ground defense plans for much of Northern Europe (including West Germany, Denmark, and Norway). During these three years in Oslo, Hal and Julie became fairly fluent in Norwegian, sent their children to Norwegian schools, and even welcomed a fifth child, David, born in March 1961. And, just as he had done in Occupied Japan, Moore found plenty of time to hit the slopes for some cross-country skiing.[84]

For Moore's young children, however, moving to Norway was a culture shock like none other. Steve Moore recalled, "When we got off the boat in Norway, I was stunned to discover that English was not the language of the world and people were speaking in gibberish. Despite that confusion, Dad enrolled Greg and I in a Norwegian Catholic school in the center of downtown Oslo. To get there, we had to walk from our home to the train station, take the train to the center of the city, and then walk a significant distance to get to the school—all at the ages of eight and nine. As I remember, we did not think anything of this . . . just that it was normal and expected. In other words, Dad instilled the confidence in us that we could do this without a problem. I still remember my first day at the school with crystal clarity: my first class was French, taught in Norwegian, to a kid who could speak neither. Thankfully, the nuns tutored Greg and I over the next several months in Norwegian and we rapidly became fluent."[85]

A few months later, Greg was playing with some of his newfound Norwegian friends when they were approached by a group of American tourists. In broken Norwegian, they attempted to ask the children for directions. Realizing that these tourists were speaking English, the children began chanting "Gregory! Gregory!" Greg walked over and addressed the startled tourists in perfect English. As he sent them on their way, he heard them comment on how a young "Norwegian" boy could speak English so well and without an accent.

While Julie, Cecile, and newborn David would often stay indoors, Greg and Steve followed their father's footsteps into the world of cross-country skiing. "Skis were the gift of choice on our first Christmas there [in Norway]," said Steve, "and, shortly thereafter, we were on the innumerable, cross-country ski trails that wind like ribbons through the dense woods that create the perimeter of Oslo. Greg and I would take the train up into the surrounding mountains and proceed to ski, by ourselves, through the surrounding wilderness. We didn't think anything of this, although I can't imagine in today's world allowing children as young as that to wander through the woods on their own.

"Cross-country skiing in Norway was a big deal," Steve continued, "and you could compete for distance skiing awards. On every trail there was a set of rubber stamps that would allow the skier to confirm on a scorecard that they had gone the appropriate distance. Dad enrolled us in the program and Greg and I skied enough in a single winter to earn the Norwegian Ski Association's gold lapel pin for skiing over 500 kilometers. As far as we know, we were the youngest Americans ever to achieve that distinction. The bottom line is that Dad instilled the self-confidence and will to win in us at an early age—just as he did in every unit he commanded."[86]

During Moore's absence overseas, President Kennedy took a fresh look at the airmobility concept. In 1962, at the behest of Secretary of Defense Robert McNamara, the Army convened the Tactical Mobility Requirements Board at Fort Bragg. Headed by General Hamilton Howze, the board's mission was to test the viability of integrating helicopters into the Army's tactical formations. After some deliberation, the board recommended creating an airmobile "test" division equipped with 459 helicopters. This new division would include airmobile infantry battalions and an air cavalry squadron to provide aerial reconnaissance and close air support. For the occasion, the Army reactivated the 11th Airborne Division in February 1963 and re-designated it the 11th Air Assault Division (Test).

"The 11th Air Assault," Hal remembered, "began at the bottom and built upward, starting with only three thousand men for individual airmobility training and testing in platoon-sized and company-sized elements. By June of 1964, the Army added two more brigades of infantry, plus artillery and support units, and began training and testing battalion, brigade, and division-level tactics." That fall, the 11th Air Assault Division conducted two massive field exercises in the Carolinas. Attended by senior Army leaders and defense planners, Air Assault I and II validated Gavin's theory of helicopter warfare, and the 11th Air Assault Division was then fully integrated into the Army force structure.[87]

Meanwhile, the situation in Vietnam had steadily gone from bad to worse. After the French were defeated at Dien Bien Phu in 1954, peace negotiations at the Geneva Conference separated Vietnam into two political entities: a northern zone, governed by the Communist Viet Minh, and a southern zone, which became the Republic of Vietnam.

Per the Geneva Accords, the Republic of Vietnam was to hold an election to decide on the option of reunification in 1956. However, Ngo Dinh Diem, the South Vietnamese President, cancelled the elections and vowed to stamp out any lingering Communists in the Republic of Vietnam. The Viet Minh who remained in the south (the first incarnation of the Viet Cong) reciprocated by launching a low-level insurgency in 1957.

After the French withdrew from Vietnam, MAAG stepped in to assist Diem in his anti-Communist efforts. The US advisory mission continued into the early 1960s until the insurgency grew to a level which Washington could no longer ignore. In 1964, MAAG was dissolved into the newly-created Military Assistance Command, Vietnam (MACV)—thereby giving the US a wider berth to send conventional forces to Southeast Asia. Almost simultaneously, President Kennedy lost his confidence in Diem's ability to rule South Vietnam. On November 2, 1963, just weeks before Kennedy's own assassination, Ngo Dinh Diem was deposed and murdered in a coup d'état which Moore characterized as being "at least sanctioned, if not sponsored, by Washington."[88]

With Diem now out of the way, the Hanoi government felt it was time to escalate the war and "liberate" South Vietnam. "They argued that simply to

Moore standing in front of a Norwegian Army snowmobile near Oslo, 1960. Moore served a three-year tour in Norway as a NATO attaché with Allied Forces–Northern Europe. *The Hal Moore Collection*

continue to provide guns and ammunition and encouragement to the Viet Cong guerrillas was not enough. The time had come to intervene on the battlefields of the south with regiments and divisions of North Vietnamese People's Army regulars. These better-armed, trained, and motivated soldiers should infiltrate South Vietnam, they argued, and launch hammer blows against the weak and unmotivated South Vietnamese army."[89]

Senior General Vo Nguyen Giap, however, opposed the plan, saying that an invasion of the south would be premature. The guerrilla war, he argued, was making excellent progress and should be allowed to carry on for the next few years without North Vietnamese regulars. Ho Chi Minh, however, strongly supported the escalation and drew up an invasion plan for the fall of 1965. The plan called for three army regiments to infiltrate the Central Highlands through the Ho Chi Minh Trail in Laos.

"They would lay siege to the American Special Forces Camp at Plei Me. That attack, in turn, would draw in an ARVN [Army of the Republic of Vietnam] relief column of troops and tanks out of Pleiku down Route 14, thence southwest on the one-lane dirt track called Provincial Route 5—where a regiment of People's Army troops would be waiting in a carefully prepared ambush." After the Plei Me Camp and the ARVN relief column had been destroyed, the North Vietnamese Army (NVA) would then head east along Route 19 to the South China Sea and the Coastal Plains. This maneuver would split South Vietnam in half and give the NVA complete control of the Central Highlands. As Hal summarized it, "Whoever controls the Highlands controls Vietnam." The North Vietnamese were confident that their jungle blitzkrieg would have South Vietnam on the verge of surrender by early 1966.[90]

Returning stateside from Europe, Moore was selected to attend the Naval War College in Providence, Rhode Island. Although the college was nominally for Naval and Marine officers, a small number of Army and Air Force personnel could also attend. During his course of study, Moore learned that Harry WO Kinnard, his old commander from the Airborne Test Section at Fort Bragg, had taken command of the new airmobile division. Moore was certain that Kinnard would remember him; after Moore's death-defying first jump in 1948, Kinnard had given him the nickname "Lucky." Excited that the airmobile concept was coming to fruition, and wanting to get in on the ground floor, Hal wrote a letter to his old boss requesting an assignment as a battalion commander. In those days, a division commander could hand-pick his own battalion commanders.[91]

After several months, Moore heard nothing back from Kinnard and prepared to take on another assignment at the Pentagon. But in April 1964, while finishing his studies at the War College, "the Pentagon informed me that Kinnard had requested that I be assigned to command the Second Battalion, 23rd Infantry, which had been detached from the 2nd Infantry Division and assigned to the 11th Air Assault Test."[92]

Moore arrived at Fort Benning on Saturday, June 27, 1964. He was excited; for it was the first time since Korea that he would have the opportunity to command troops. Although he had expected to take the five-day, pre-command course, his new boss, the 3rd Brigade commander, Colonel Thomas W. "Tim" Brown told him otherwise: "You take command of your battalion at nine a.m. Monday and we are going out on a three-day field exercise right after."[93]

Before his change-of-command ceremony, however, Moore met the most memorable NCO of his career—Sergeant Major Basil L. Plumley. In Moore's own words, Plumley was "the very essence of an airborne soldier"— six foot two, squared-jawed, with a crew cut and a penetrating stare. He had made all four combat jumps with the 82nd Airborne Division in World War II—Sicily, Salerno, D-Day, and Market Garden—plus one more in Korea with the 187th Regimental Combat Team. Paying his dues as a platoon sergeant and company first sergeant in West Germany, he had risen steadily through the enlisted ranks and was promoted to Sergeant Major in 1961.[94]

"I liked the man immediately," Moore said, "and it turned out that we thought a lot alike when it came to soldiering and leading soldiers in training . . . and in battle." During their first meeting, Moore told Plumley that the Sergeant Major had unlimited access to him at any time. Plumley would personally oversee the professional development of the battalion's NCOs. In the matter of disciplining the troops for misconduct, Moore would always ask for Plumley's recommendation before administering punishment.[95]

But as Moore admitted, "the Sergeant Major was very ornery." He was dead-honest and blunt to the point where he "scared the hell out of the troopers." Some of the troops even speculated that God himself looked like the Sergeant Major. Plumley also had a reputation for being an intensely private person. Whenever asked about the details of his life and service, his response was always the same: "I don't do interviews." What little is known about

Moore with his fellow Army students at the Naval War College, 1964. *The Hal Moore Collection*

Plumley comes from official Army records or the personal recollections of those who have served with him. His enlistment record indicates that he was born on January 1, 1920 in Bluejay, West Virginia. Growing up during the Great Depression, he once said that he joined the Army simply because it was "better than starving to death." Attracted to the novelty of the Airborne Corps, Plumley volunteered for the paratroops in August 1942 and deployed to Europe the following year. During his service in World War II and Korea, he had earned a Silver Star and picked up three Purple Hearts.[96]

At the change-of-command ceremony, Moore told his new battalion how proud he was to be their commander. They were on the cutting edge of a new doctrine, new tactics, and—with intense training—things could only get better. "I will do my best," he told them, "and I expect the same from you." After the ceremony, Hal met with the battalion's officers to discuss his standards and expectations. "Only first place trophies will be displayed, accepted, or presented in this battalion," he said. "Second place in our line of work is defeat of the unit on the battlefield, and death for the individual in combat. No fat troops or officers. Decision-making will be decentralized: push the power down. It pays off in wartime. Loyalty flows down as well. I check up on everything. I am available day or night to talk with any officer in the battalion."

Finally, Hal emphasized that the Sergeant Major answered only to him.[97]

When Moore took command, his goal was to create the best air assault battalion in the Army. And he wanted his troopers to feel the same way. He instituted some tough training and tough standards for his men, but remembered to show compassion in his leadership.

One on occasion, only a few months into his command, a young private lost his rifle during a field exercise. This was shortly after the M-16 assault rifle had been issued throughout the Army. Although lightweight, durable, and capable of automatic fire, many soldiers derisively called it the "Mattel toy," since many of its features were made of hard plastic. During this three-day field operation, the clever young private decided that he could turn his inflatable bedroll into a raft and drift up the Upatoi Creek to a rendezvous point instead of having to make the foot march there. The makeshift raft accomplished its mission but, en route, the soldier's rifle slipped out of its harness and landed somewhere in the creek. The private didn't even realize his weapon was missing until after he had come ashore.[98]

The young soldier confessed his mistake to his squad leader and company commander, who then brought the trooper to see Lieutenant Colonel Moore. Normally, losing one's rifle was an Article 15 offense (non-judicial punishment) and included forfeiture of pay equal to the cost of the missing weapon. But rather than berate the soldier, Moore simply commanded him to fix the problem. "Well, you boys are going to get in that creek and you're going to walk it. I don't care how long it takes until you find that missing rifle. We're all going back to base, but I will have a fresh supply of C-Rations brought out to you. Have a good hunt!" It was a Friday evening and the entire battalion was set to return to base for the weekend—except for the errant private and his squad.[99]

It was a tough lesson, but Moore knew it was better to make the private find his weapon than to take his pay and make him feel worse than he already did. It reinforced everything he held dear about leadership and building loyalty—"never do anything that takes away from the self-respect of the person." Although it took his squad the entire weekend, the soldier eventually found his rifle buried in the mud of the Upatoi.

The workhorse of the 11th Air Assault was the Bell UH-1 "Huey" helicopter. Its sleek design and the distinctive *whoop-whoop-whoop* sound of its rotor blades made it an icon of the Vietnam War. Within these newly designed helicopters, Hal Moore trained his battalion in the art of airmobile warfare. Because the tactics were new, they often lent themselves to trial and error. Heliborne commanders had much more to deal with than their ground-based counterparts. For instance, they had to coordinate artillery strikes within the time frames of their helicopter landings. One miscalculation, or ill-timed radio call, could send an artillery round into a row of helicopters while they were still in flight. Airmobile commanders also had to look at the terrain in terms of selecting potential landing zones (LZs) and pickup zones (PZs).

"We practiced rapid loading and unloading of men and materiel to reduce the helicopters window of vulnerability. Total flexibility was the watchword in planning and attitude." It worked out well because these air assault mission gave the soldiers more time to fight and saved them the energy which would otherwise be spent walking.[100]

Nevertheless, Moore insisted that the training be as realistic as possible. He wanted every man in the battalion to prepare for the worst-case scenario. During training, Moore said "we would often declare a platoon leader dead and let his sergeant take over and carry out the mission." On other occasions, he would declare a squad leader dead and have one of his privates take over. The goal was to have every man learn the job of the man above him. After all, "we were training for war, and leaders are killed in battle."[101]

In the opening months of Moore's command, the 11th Air Assault participated in a number of airmobile exercises, including Air Assault I, Hawk Star I, and the culminating Air Assault II. It was during Air Assault II that the division underwent its final testing and validation. "Some 35,000 soldiers were involved; the 11th Air Assault Division was pitted against the 'aggressor' forces, the 82nd Airborne Division," Moore recalled. "Hundreds of VIPs from Washington popped in and out to see helicopter warfare in action; their presence gave rise to the first round of rumors that we were being trained for duty in Vietnam." Ironically, during that same exercise, the radio in Moore's battalion command post picked up some radio traffic from a firefight in Vietnam. "We could hear the rattle of gunfire and the explosions of the bombs twelve thousand miles away on a freak bounce of radio waves that briefly brought the real war to the pine barrens of South Carolina where we were playing war games."[102]

Throughout 1964, Moore's battalion operated at or near its full strength—767 men. However, in the spring of 1965, his most seasoned officers began transferring out of the battalion. Some were Reserve officers whose obligatory, two-year active duty tour had come to an end. Others were simply reassigned elsewhere. That spring and summer, "we lost eight of our fifteen platoon leader lieutenants . . . our intelligence officer, surgeon, personnel officer, air operations officer, supply officer, assistant medical officer, chaplain, and two company commanders."[103]

The following June, six of the eight reassigned platoon leaders were replaced by a fresh contingent from West Point and ROTC. Moore gave each of them a platoon leader position and a seven-week crash course in air assault tactics. However, a few weeks before the unit deployed, these six new lieutenants were suddenly withdrawn from the unit. Apparently, none of them had attended the Infantry Officer Basic Course yet; and per Army policy, no lieutenant could deploy to a combat zone without first attending the course. "The policy may be sound," Moore admitted, "but the net result was that the battalion and the troops in the ranks were whipsawed by unnecessary leadership changes."[104]

As Moore and his soldiers perfected the air assault technique, the powder keg in Vietnam finally exploded. In the wake of Diem's assassination, Saigon went through a series of violent coups d'état staged by South Vietnamese generals who took turns being "strongman of the month." Meanwhile, the Viet

Moore's first command portrait as the CO of 2nd Battalion, 23rd Infantry. Moore's battalion was initially part of the 11th Air Assault Division, the first airmobile division in the US Army. The 11th Air Assault Division was later redesignated the 1st Cavalry Division (Airmobile). Moore's battalion then became the 1st Battalion, 7th Cavalry. *The Ballard Moore Collection*

Moore takes a moment to relax with daughters Cecile (left) and Julie (right) at the family's new abode in Fort Benning, Georgia, 1964. *The Hal Moore Collection*

Cong continued to grow in the Mekong Delta and began exerting their influence in the Central Highlands and the Coastal Plains. In the middle of it all, the ARVN remained poorly led and largely unmotivated.[105]

In August 1964, Congress passed the infamous Gulf of Tonkin Resolution. The new law was drafted in response to a naval skirmish involving North Vietnamese boats and the US destroyers *Maddox* and *C. Turner Joy*. Essentially, it gave President Lyndon Johnson the unprecedented authority to use conventional military force in Vietnam without a formal declaration of war. Still, Johnson was confident that he could "cut a deal in the best Texas tradition with the Vietnamese Communists."[106]

All that changed, however, on the night of February 15, 1965, when Viet Cong sappers attacked the US airbase at Pleiku. That night, a fed-up Johnson went to his National Security Council and said, "I've had enough of this." The following month, he authorized a systematic bombing campaign, and on March 8, 1965, the first US Marines waded ashore at Da Nang. Meanwhile, the new MACV commander, General William C. Westmoreland, continued pressing Johnson for more troops. By Westmoreland's estimate, he would need nearly 180,000 troops by the end of 1965.[107]

This was a bit unsettling for Johnson, who had wanted to pursue the war in Vietnam without detracting from his Great Society programs. After all, a country as rich and powerful as the United States shouldn't have to choose between guns and butter. Thus, in another bad decision for America's war ef-

Major General Harry WO Kinnard salutes his troops during a farewell ceremony for the 1st Cavalry Division (Airmobile) at Lawson Army Airfield, adjacent to Fort Benning. August 13, 1965.
The Columbus Ledger Enquirer

fort, Johnson ignored the advice of his military chiefs and decided that "the American escalation in South Vietnam could be conducted on the cheap." There would be no mobilization of the Reserve or National Guard; and no declared state of emergency, which would have allowed the army to extend the enlistments of its best-trained troops. "Instead, the war would be fed by stripping the Army divisions in Europe and the continental United States of their best personnel and materiel, while a river of new draftees, 20,000 of them each month, flowed in to do the shooting and the dying."[108]

In the months that followed, the brigade and battalion commanders of the 11th Air Assault Division began receiving after-action reports from the 173rd Airborne Brigade's operations in Vietnam. Devouring these reports, the commanders and staff at Fort Benning were soon conducting top-secret map exercises on overlays of the Central Highlands. "By mid-June," Hal said, "the Pentagon ordered the division commanders to begin an intensive eight-week combat readiness program that focused on deployment to South Vietnam."[109]

Following these developments, it came as no surprise when, on July 28, 1965, President Johnson made the following announcement on national television:

We intend to convince the Communists that we cannot be defeated by a force of arms. I have asked the commanding general, General Westmoreland, what more he needs to meet this mounting aggression. He has told me. And we will meet his needs. I have today ordered to Vietnam the Airmobile Division, and certain other forces which raise our fighting strength from 75,000 to 125,000.

That month, the Pentagon also announced that the 11th Air Assault Division would be re-flagged as the 1st Cavalry Division (Airmobile).

Almost immediately, Hal's brigade commander asked that his two battalions be given the colors of the 7th Cavalry Regiment. Moore's battalion then became the 1st Battalion, 7th Cavalry. Their sister unit was designated the 2nd Battalion, 7th Cavalry. "In the days when Lieutenant Colonel George Armstrong Custer commanded the 7th Cavalry, the regiment adopted a rowdy Irish drinking song, 'Garry Owen,' as its marching tune." The song title soon became the official motto of the regiment and the men customarily greeted their officers with a salute and a cheery, "Garry Owen, sir!"[110]

Unfortunately, Moore's battalion continued to suffer under Johnson's personnel policies. The President's refusal to declare a state of emergency meant that draftees or Reserve officers could not have their active duty tours extended to meet the deployment date. In fact, any soldier who was within sixty days of the end of his enlistment by August 16, 1965, had to be left behind.

"We were sick at heart," Hal said. "We were being shipped off to war sadly under-strength and crippled by the loss of a hundred troopers in my battalion alone. The very men who would be the most useful in combat—those who had trained the longest in the new techniques of helicopter warfare—were by this order taken away from us. It made no sense then; it makes no sense now."[111]

Just before Hal's departure from Fort Benning, his youngest brother, Ballard—who had become a world-class tennis coach—stopped by for a visit while on his way to Florida. Over a game of tennis, Ballard said, "Hal, that's a rough gig, having to go to Vietnam."

"Well, little brother," Hal replied, "it's the only goddamn war we've got right now."[112]

1-7 Cavalry soldiers performing PT on the deck on the USNS *Maurice Rose* en route to Vietnam, August 1965. *The Hal Moore Collection*

CHAPTER FIVE

IA DRANG

O n his last night at Fort Benning—August 13, 1965—Moore gathered his five children around the dinner table. Greg, the eldest, was now thirteen, and his youngest child, David, had recently turned three. He told all of them that he would be leaving early the next morning, and that he would be going to the war in Vietnam. Later that evening, as Moore sat reading a storybook to his daughter Cecile, age six, she looked up at him and asked: "Daddy, what's a war?" He paused for a moment, and although he tried to explain, "her look of bewilderment only grew."[113]

He rose at 1:30 a.m. the following morning and by 3:30 a.m., his battalion had loaded aboard a fleet of charter buses headed for Charleston, South Carolina, where the USNS *Maurice Rose* lay waiting to take them to Vietnam. Moore's battalion sailed from Charleston on August 16 and, through the confines of the Panama Canal, they crossed the Pacific to the shores of South Vietnam. "On that same date, August 16, the last elements of the 66th Regiment of the People's Army left their base in Thanh Hoa, North Vietnam. It would take them nearly two months to cover five hundred miles on foot along the Ho Chi Minh Trail to our meeting place in the Ia Drang Valley."[114]

One month later, the "Ramblin' Rose" dropped her anchor at the port of Qui Nhon. Prior to the battalion's arrival, the 101st Airborne had secured a large swath of jungle north of An Khe. The area would become the base camp for the 1st Cavalry Division—"just as soon as we cleared the jungle and built that camp." Although the area was nominally "secure," An Khe had been precisely what General Kinnard *didn't* want. He had requested, on numerous occasions, a base camp in Thailand, where his troopers could launch attacks against the NVA operating in Laos and Cambodia. "The negative responses

General Kinnard's requests elicited weren't even polite," Moore said. "His division would now have to build, garrison, and guard a base camp and that would reduce the number of troops available to actively pursue and destroy the enemy."[115]

The site for the An Khe base camp was a tangled mess of trees and brush. The Assistant Division Commander for Support, General John M. Wright, remarked that he wanted the camp area to be as "smooth as a golf course." This meant that the troopers would have to clear the site by hand. Bulldozers were not allowed—if the division stirred up the red topsoil, the entire camp would become a mud hole during the monsoon season.[116]

Some two thousand Vietnamese laborers were brought in to assist the division in clearing the land. With axes and machetes, they spent the next few weeks building General Wright's "golf course" campsite. They also built a twelve-mile-long defensive perimeter around the base. Referred to as the "Barrier Line," the perimeter was a massive structure, one hundred yards deep and reinforced with sandbags, concertina wire, and watch towers. "We lived rough," Moore said, sleeping in pup tents and surviving on a diet of canned C-Rations. Each of the battalions, including Moore's, took turns patrolling the perimeter. During the first few days at An Khe, there were a few probes from the local guerrillas and Moore recalled that his young troopers nervously fired at any sound that came from beyond the perimeter.[117]

Sadly, one of the first casualties from these nervous perimeter guards was the 1-9 Cavalry's mascot, Maggie the Mule. She had been gunned down by a Charlie Company sentry as she wandered the perimeter at night. Sergeant Major Plumley reported the mule's death with his customary dry wit: "She was challenged and she didn't know the password." Plumley then gave his word that he would "properly dispose" of the body. His idea of a proper disposal, however, was to tie the slain mule to the back of a division food truck. While making its morning deliveries, the truck unloaded Maggie's body at the 1-9 Cavalry command post, right alongside their delivery of the battalion's C-Rations. "Hardly a diplomatic solution," Moore noted.[118]

As the Vietnamese summer turned to fall, Moore and his men continued to acclimate themselves to the jungle environment. Every day, he and his men took malaria pills and slept under the cover of near-suffocating mosquito nets. Yet despite these countermeasures, fifty-six of his troopers caught malaria within the first few weeks. All were evacuated to nearby field hospitals.

Above: Moore's troopers display
their decorative artwork aboard
the Maurice Rose as the ship
steams closer to Vietnam.
The Hal Moore Collection

Right: Hal Moore and Sergeant
Major Basil Plumley outside the
battalion's base camp in South
Vietnam, October 1965.
The Hal Moore Collection

Meanwhile, Moore's battalion continued to suffer under the Army's dubious personnel policies. Because the President still refused to declare a state of emergency, any soldier whose enlistment expired while overseas had the option to return home. "At the end of September, my battalion had 679 officers and men against an authorized strength of 767"—and the expiring enlistments drained his manpower even further. In October, he lost four sergeants and seventeen men when their service obligations ended. The following month, 138 rotated home.[119]

In light of these losses, however, Moore did gain two new officers from the so-called "infusion program"—which transferred officers already serving in Vietnam to incoming units. Under this program, Moore received Captain Thomas M. Metsker and First Lieutenant William J. Lyons. Metsker was a Special Forces officer and a 1961 graduate of the Citadel. Lyons, a twenty-five-year-old paratrooper and Vietnamese linguist, had been a US advisor to an ARVN Ranger battalion. Metsker became the battalion Intelligence Officer (S-2) while Lyons was sent to Charlie Company as their Executive Officer. Sadly, Lyons was killed in a head-on collision between two helicopters on November 4.

Throughout October, 1-7 Cavalry conducted two combat patrols outside the perimeter of An Khe. Although relatively uneventful in Moore's sector, enemy activity was on the rise elsewhere in Pleiku province. On November 1, Lieutenant Colonel Stockton's 1-9 Cavalry traded fire with North Vietnamese regulars eight miles west of Plei Me. During this engagement, 1-9 captured the 33rd NVA Regiment's field hospital. "Fifteen enemy were killed and forty-four others, including patients and hospital staff, were captured along with medical supplies, rice, documents, and weapons." That same day, lead elements of the 66th NVA Regiment crossed into South Vietnam from Cambodia and began making their way down the Ia Drang River.[120]

Meanwhile, the documents obtained from the captured hospital revealed the vast trail network that the enemy had been using throughout the Ia Drang Valley. Armed with this information, General Knowles, the Assistant Division Commander for Maneuver, directed Stockon's 1-9 Cavalry to conduct a reconnaissance in force along the main trail running from the Cambodian border. Stockton set a series of ambushes along that trail, which resulted in a number of heavy firefights with NVA regulars.

Surprisingly, though, "division headquarters did not at that time move to exploit the success of Stockton's ambush," Moore said, "and pursue the con-

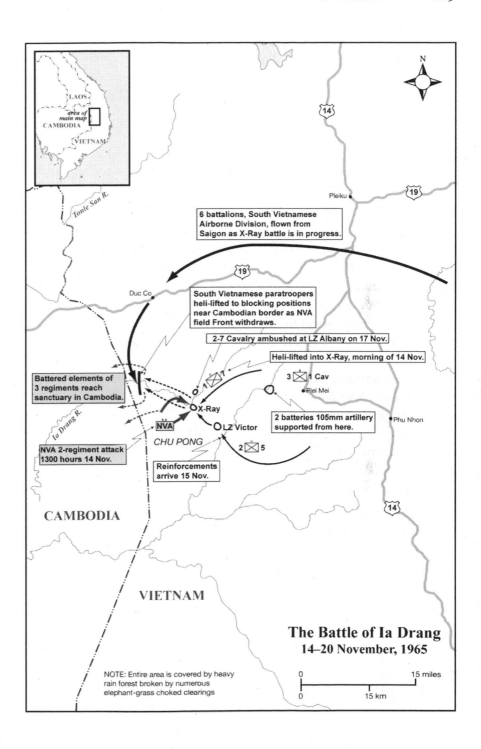

6 battalions, South Vietnamese Airborne Division, flown from Saigon as X-Ray battle is in progress.

South Vietnamese paratroopers heli-lifted to blocking positions near Cambodian border as NVA field Front withdraws.

2-7 Cavalry ambushed at LZ Albany on 17 Nov.

Heli-lifted into X-Ray, morning of 14 Nov.

3 ⊠ 1 Cav

Battered elements of 3 regiments reach sanctuary in Cambodia.

2 batteries 105mm artillery supported from here.

NVA

NVA 2-regiment attack 1300 hours 14 Nov.

CHU PONG

2 ⊠ 5

Reinforcements arrive 15 Nov.

CAMBODIA

VIETNAM

The Battle of Ia Drang
14–20 November, 1965

NOTE: Entire area is covered by heavy rain forest broken by numerous elephant-grass choked clearings

0   15 miles

0   15 km

LAOS
area of main map
CAMBODIA
VIETNAM

Tonle San R.

Pleiku

Duc Co

Plei Mei

Phu Nhon

X-Ray

LZ Victor

Ia Drang R.

3rd Brigade
Headquarters at
the 1st Cavalry
Division camp
near An Khe,
looking east.
*The Hal Moore
Collection*

siderable number of enemy reinforcements who had just arrived off the Ho
Chi Minh Trail. Instead, on November 6, orders were issued for the 1st
Brigade to return to An Khe and for 3rd Brigade to take the field in Pleiku
province, effective November 10. The 3rd Brigade battalions were under
Colonel Tim Brown, and included my 1st Battalion, 7th Cavalry; Lieutenant
Colonel Robert McDade's 2nd Battalion, 7th Cavalry; and Lieutenant Colonel
Robert Tully's 2nd Battalion, 5th Cavalry. McDade, a Korean War veteran had
been the Division Personnel Officer (G-1) for nearly two years and had been
given command of our sister battalion in late October."[121]

On the morning of November 9, Moore accompanied Colonel Brown to
the division's forward command post for an update on the enemy situation.
"The intelligence map hanging on the wall had a large red star on the Chu
Pong massif above the Ia Drang Valley, west of Plei Me. I asked one of the
briefers what significance the star had, and he replied: 'Enemy base camp.'
The next day my battalion was flown from An Khe to brigade field headquarters at the Catecka Tea Plantation, where Colonel Brown's staff briefed us and
gave me my mission: to conduct an air assault mission, five miles *east* of Plei
Me, and find and kill the enemy." Moore was surprised. Thus far, all of the
division's contact with the enemy had been *west* of Plei Me. Yet his battalion
was being ordered to assault in the opposite direction. "Then there was that
big red star on the intelligence map, which indicated that the biggest target
of all was way out west."[122]

Before their air assault into the target area, Moore and his Battalion S-3,
Captain Gregory "Matt" Dillon conducted a low-altitude reconnaissance of

the area. Dillon was an ROTC graduate from the University of Alabama and had commanded the battalion's Bravo Company before moving into the S-3 office.

During their flight, the pair spotted a small Montagnard village. The term Montagnard (French for "mountain people") referred to the various tribes which inhabited the Central Highlands of Vietnam. Primitive and largely agrarian, the Montagnard had had little contact with the outside world other than with the French Catholic missionaries. Since the early 1960s, however, Americans had been building relationships with the Montagnard because their tribal lands bordered the area of the Ho Chi Minh Trail. The US military would go on to recruit some 40,000 Montagnards throughout the war, many of whom fought alongside the Americans in their effort to halt the Communist infiltration from Laos and Cambodia.

Because there were friendly (or at least neutral) civilians on the ground, Moore decided not to prep the area with an artillery strike ahead of the helicopter landings. Moore's helicopters were already intruding on their farmlands; he saw no use in pummeling their crops with 105mm gunfire, too.

An aerial view of the 1st Cavalry Division's base camp and its fleet of Huey helicopters.
The Hal Moore Collection

"We shuttled the battalion in on sixteen Huey troop-transport choppers," Moore said. Moore and Plumley landed in the first wave along with Alpha Company under the command of Captain Ramon "Tony" Nadal. Nadal was one of Moore's most experienced officers; he had already spent a year in Vietnam commanding a Special Forces A-Team. There was no enemy on the field, but nearly half-a-dozen Montagnards—all of whom scattered when the helicopters touched down. "For the next two and half days, we ran small unit patrols throughout the area," but still had no enemy contact. Every so often, they would pass a Montagnard settlement and, on one occasion, a village elder greeted them wearing a tattered French Army tunic and carrying a small French tricolor flag. Apparently, the old man thought Moore and his troopers were returning Frenchmen.[123]

During this patrol, Moore became well acquainted with UPI reporter Joe Galloway, a twenty-three-year-old native of Refugio, Texas. Galloway was one of several American reporters embedded with US ground forces, and had previously covered the Marines at Da Nang. "My first time out with Hal Moore's 1st Battalion, 7th Cavalry," he remembered, "was a hellish walk in the sun to a remote Montagnard mountain village. We got into a patch of brush and wait-a-minute vines so thick and thorny that every step had to be carved out with machetes. We covered maybe three hundred yards in four hours, and forded a fast-running chest-deep mountain stream just as darkness fell, then huddled in our ponchos, wet and freezing, all night long."[124]

The following morning, Galloway pinched off a piece of C-4 explosive and used it to boil some water for his morning cup of coffee. Using C-4 like this was a very delicate matter. "If you lit the C-4 carefully," Joe said, "you could be drinking hot coffee in maybe thirty seconds; if you were careless, it blew your arm off." Over his morning cigarette, Galloway noticed Moore's men were shaving. "Shaving? Up here?" he thought. Galloway was impressed. Then Moore came over to him and said, "We all shave in my outfit—reporters included." Without hesitation, Galloway's steaming coffee water went towards his morning shave. "I gained a measure of respect for the man."[125]

The battalion continued patrolling to the south and east, but grew more frustrated as there were no Viet Cong or NVA in the area. Finally, General Knowles flew into the area to see how things were going for his eastward patrols. Colonel Brown wasted no time: "Dry hole, sir." Moore, who was with Brown at the time, concurred. "Nothing here, General, we're just wearing out the troops." Knowles turned to Brown and asked: "Tim, what do you think about heading west—a long jump into the Ia Drang Valley?" Brown agreed. After all, division intelligence had suggested that the enemy was really out west.[126]

Knowles gave Brown the go-ahead while Moore told his staff to begin a map study of the Ia Drang Valley. "I had no doubt," Moore said, "that my battalion would be chosen to mount the attack into the Ia Drang." The following afternoon, November 13, his hunch proved correct. "Hal, I'm moving your battalion west tomorrow morning," Colonel Brown said as he pulled out his map. "Here is your area of operations—north of Chu Pong in the Ia Drang Valley. Your mission is the same one you have now: Find and kill the enemy."[127]

Just as before, Moore would have sixteen helicopters at his disposal for the assault into Ia Drang. Two 105mm howitzer batteries would support the operation from Firebase Falcon. Brown added that Alpha Company from the 229th Assault Helicopter Battalion would provide the choppers. Their company commander, Major Bruce Crandall, went by the call sign "Ancient Serpent 6" but he was more often referred to as "Old Snake" or "Snakeshit 6." Although none of his aircrews had seen combat, they were the best group of helicopter pilots the Army had to offer. "Old Snake" drove his men hard and enforced the same high standards on everyone. Crandall said that "what we lacked in experience, we made up for in flying time." Indeed, even the most junior pilot in his company had about 700 hours of flight time.[128]

As Moore flew back to his battalion command post, "I jotted notes on what needed to be done and radioed Matt Dillon, my operations officer, telling him to put out a warning order to the other company commanders and support units and get the staff together." From that point forward, they had less than twenty-four hours to plan their assault into the Ia Drang Valley.

Time was of the essence, but Hal made the best use of it. He integrated Crandall and his pilots into the battalion and forced their attendance at every planning and analysis meetings. Crandall later remarked, "As a team, we proved that the whole was even better than the sum of the parts."[129]

At the 1-7 command post, Moore and his staff poured over the details of the operation. Topics such as terrain, potential landing zones, enemy manpower, weather forecasts, and logistics were all part of the equation in Moore's battlefield calculus. Crandall's sixteen helicopters would arrive at Plei Me by 9:30 a.m. to deliver the first wave of troops into battle. Hal ordered an early morning recon flight over Ia Drang in case anything on the ground was different than what division intelligence had predicted. Bravo Company, under

An aerial view of LZ X-Ray from Moore's helicopter, facing southwest.
The Hal Moore Collection

2-7 Cavalry soldiers at Camp Holloway, Pleiku, November 1965. *The Hal Moore Collection*

A lone Chinook helicopter stands against the sunset at the An Khe base camp, October 29, 1965. The Chinook was a "stable mate" to the UH-1 Huey, and served as a cargo carrier, troop transport, and recovery helicopter. *Photo by MB Alford. The Hal Moore Collection*

LZ X-Ray, Ia Drang Valley, VietNam. Chu Pong Massif in Background Sunday, 14 Nov. 1965 Approx. 1330 hrs.

LZ X-Ray on November 14, 1965 at approximately 1:30 p.m. Smoke can be seen rising from the LZ as the firefight between the Americans and North Vietnamese becomes more intense. *The Hal Moore Collection* the command of Captain John Herren, would be the lead element during the initial assault. "Plan for a twenty-minute artillery prep followed by thirty seconds of aerial rocket artillery, then thirty seconds by the gunships," he told his commanders and staff.[130]

It was 8:00 p.m. when the meeting at the command post broke for the night. "Sergeant Major Plumley and I ate and then walked around the inner perimeter of the old French fort, occasionally climbing the dirt berms to peer out into the darkness. I felt strongly that the enemy had been using the Ia Drang Valley as a jumping-off point for the attacks on Plei Me and likely had returned there to regroup and treat their wounded. The Ia Drang had plenty of water for drinking and for cooking rice. Best of all . . . was its location on the border with Cambodia. The Vietnamese Communists came and went across that border at will; we were prohibited from crossing it. The intelligence people were telling me their best guess: possibly one battalion at the base of the Chu Pong massif two miles northwest of the area we were aiming for; possibly enemy very near a clearing we were considering for the assault landing zone; and a possible secret base a half-mile east of our target area. If even one of those possibles was an *actual*, we would get a violent response."[131]

Moore then thought about his troopers. "We had never maneuvered in combat as an entire battalion, although all three rifle companies had been in minor scrapes. Most of the men had never seen an enemy soldier, dead or alive. We had killed fewer than ten men, black-pajama guerrillas, in the get-acquainted patrols and small operations since our arrival in An Khe." Still, Moore had every confidence in his men. The more pressing issues on his mind, however, were the lingering manpower shortages. All four line companies were under-strength going into the fight. A combination of expiring enlistments, malaria, and soldiers tasked out to division had whittled his battalion to barely 450 men. "I didn't like being short-handed," Moore said, "but things had been no different in the Korean War and somehow we made do."

Furthermore, the battalion's tempo was tethered to the Huey's timetable. Moore had only sixteen helicopters for the operation. Assuming all helicopters were functional, fewer than eighty men could arrive at the battlefield in one trip. Moreover, it was a thirty minute round-trip for the helicopters, even at full gallop. The first wave of troops, therefore, would be on the ground for half an hour without reinforcements. If a Huey were lost to enemy fire, it would impact the timetable even further.

"I ran an endless string of 'what ifs' through my mind that night as I leaned against the earthen wall of the French fort. My worst-case scenario was a hot LZ—a fight beginning during or just after our assault landing—and I certainly had to assume the enemy would be able to provide it.

"I ran through what I could do to influence the action if the worst came to pass. First, I would personally land on the first helicopter, piloted by Bruce Crandall. That would permit me a final, low-level look at the landing zone and the surrounding terrain, and with Crandall in the front seat and me in the back we could work out, on the spot, any last-minute diversion to an alternate landing zone, if necessary,

A photograph taken from LZ X-Ray looking towards the Chu Pong massif. November 15, 1965. *Photo by Henry Dunn. The Hal Moore Collection*

and fix any other problems with the lift." Moore knew that a good commander had to be on the ground with his troops during the fight. It was a sacred tenet of Moore's leadership philosophy—a leader had to see the situation developing in front of him if he wanted to be effective in combat. It was too easy to be detached from the situation while sitting in a command post or circling the battlefield from 1,500 feet in a helicopter. Instead, Moore would be the first to set foot on the battlefield, followed closely thereafter by Sergeant Major Plumley. The only helicopter circling the battlefield overhead would be the one occupied by the battalion fire support team. From 2,000 feet, and with S-3 Matt Dillon coordinating, the fire support helicopter would direct all incoming artillery fires.[132]

Moore also had to maximize the impact of his first eighty men on the ground. Airmobile doctrine at the time stipulated that the lead elements would spread out to the farthest reaches of the landing zone and secure a 360 degree perimeter. "Not this time," Moore said. "I was thinking about a new technique that seemed tailor-made for this situation. Bravo Company would assemble in a central location in the landing zone as a reserve and strike force.

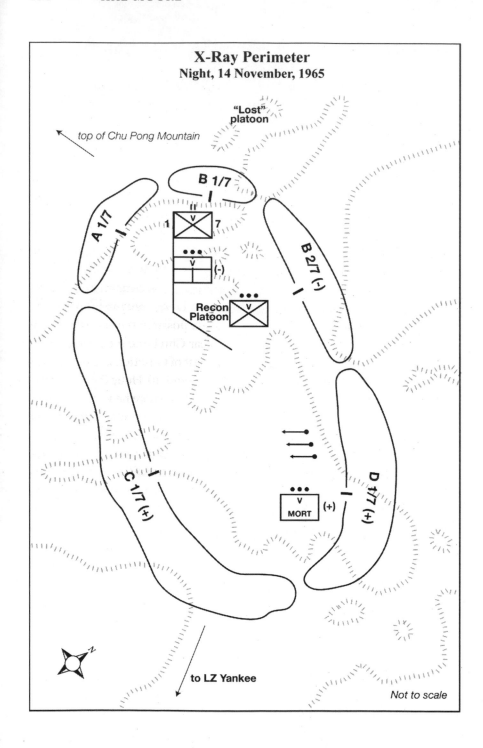

X-Ray Perimeter
Night, 14 November, 1965

"Lost" platoon

top of Chu Pong Mountain

B 1/7

A 1/7

1   7

(-)

Recon Platoon

B 2/7 (-)

C 1/7 (+)

D 1/7 (+)

MORT   (+)

N

to LZ Yankee

Not to scale

Four seven-man squads would be sent out in different directions to check out the perimeter and surrounding area."[133]

At 10:30 p.m., Moore and Plumley walked back to the command post. Rolling himself up in his poncho, Moore settled in for the last good night's sleep he would have for three days.

At 4:30 a.m. on Sunday, November 14, Moore rolled out his poncho and walked over to his operations tent, which was manned by his battle staff around the clock. Over a cup of coffee, S-3 Matt Dillon passed him a radio intercept from the night before. It was coded in Mandarin Chinese and appeared to be a situation report, "from a position somewhere on a line from Plei Me camp directly through a clearing at the base of Chu Pong mountain. The intelligence lieutenant had a map with a line drawn on it. He said that the radio transmitter was somewhere on this line. I don't remember how long that message was—that didn't really bother me. It was the direction it came from. The lieutenant said that he thought that possibly there was a North Vietnamese regiment somewhere out there near Chu Pong mountain."[134]

Moore then shaved, enjoyed a hasty breakfast of C-Rations, and gathered his ammunition before walking over to Bruce Crandall's Huey for the morning recon. Colonel Brown had told Moore generally where he wanted him to land, but now Moore had to select a landing zone, "and preferably one that would take as many of our sixteen Hueys as possible at one time.

"All of us would have preferred not to make an air-recon flight at all. We didn't want to spook the enemy in the area and possibly alert them to an imminent landing. But we could not choose a landing zone for this assault simply by looking at a 1:50,000 map; we had to overfly the area. We would minimize the chances of discovery by flying high, around 4,500 feet, and pass well to the southeast of the Chu Pong massif on a straight-line flight to the vicinity of Duc Co Special Forces camp. After orbiting the camp for five minutes we would fly a slightly different return route."[135]

All this, Moore hoped, would fool the enemy commander into thinking that the aircraft overhead was on other business. Peering from the aircraft with a pair of high-powered binoculars, Moore wanted a landing zone with the fewest obstacles and plenty of room to maneuver. The flight out to Ia Drang went as planned and when he returned to Plei Me, he had narrowed his selection down to three possible landing zones: "X-Ray, Tango, and Yankee"—so named according to letters of the NATO Phonetic Alphabet. Moore ultimately selected X-Ray. "It was flat, the trees around it weren't all that tall; and it looked as though it could take up to eight helicopters at one time." The landing zone was about the size of a football field, 100 meters in length from east to west, and it stood at the foot of the Chu Pong massif.[136]

As the battalion readied itself for the first flight into X-Ray, "I again urged the company commanders to make certain every rifleman had at least the basic load of three hundred rounds of ammo and two hand grenades plus as much additional ammunition as he felt he could carry. Each of the M-79 grenadiers should have at least thirty-six of the fat little 40mm rounds. Each squad would be carrying two of the new LAW (light anti-tank weapon) rockets for bunker-busting and taking out machine-gun crews. And I reminded the commanders of follow-on units waiting for their turn to ride into the landing zone to stay tuned to the command net and listen to what was going on so they wouldn't be in the dark about the situation at X-Ray when they finally got there."[137]

Just then, Colonel Brown arrived at the camp and Moore walked him through the details of the plan. Brown seemed satisfied with the arrangement,

Bruce Crandall steers his Huey over the LZ after delivering another wave of Moore's troopers to the battlefield. *US Army photo*

Another wave of troops touch down at LZ X-Ray, November 14, 1965. *US Army photo*

but his parting remarks left Moore and his S-3 Matt Dillon feeling unsettled. "I want you two to stay careful." Brown looked gravely concerned and slightly panic-stricken as he delivered his words.

When Colonel Brown departed, Moore gathered his landing party for the first wave onto X-Ray. They loaded aboard and, with the mechanical melody of starting propeller blades, Crandall and his pilots lifted off from Plei Me to their landing zone in the lush hills of the Ia Drang. They flew in four groups of four helicopters each, and maintained a cruising altitude of 2,000 feet to minimize the chance of being hit by small-arms fire. Piled into these sixteen helicopters were men from John Herren's Bravo Company, along with Moore, the intrepid Sergeant Major, their Montagnard interpreter, Mr. Nik, S-2 Captain Metsker, and Moore's radio operator, Specialist 4 Bob Ouellette. "About four miles from X-Ray, Bruce Crandall gave the signal and his pilots dropped down to treetop level to fly nap [near as possible]-of-the-earth on the final approach. Birds scattered as we roared along at 110 miles per hour just above their perches." Meanwhile, Dillon busied himself coordinating the artillery preparations from high above the LZ in the fire support chopper. Dillon knew that the hardest part of any air assault operation was timing the artillery ahead of the landings. Without precise calculations, a fire support officer could send a hail of artillery rounds through a helicopter formation before it even reached the LZ. Dillon also knew that if he called off the artillery fire too early, the enemy might occupy the LZ and be waiting for the choppers by the time they touched down.[138]

Dillon, however, timed the artillery strike perfectly and "cease-fired" the gun battery minutes before the first helicopter came within sight of the LZ. As Moore caught sight of X-Ray, he could tell that the artillery fire had been minimal. To hedge their bets, the Huey gunships pounded the perimeter with a cascade of rocket, grenade, and machine-gun fire, "using twenty-four of the forty-eight 2.75-inch rockets each carried. They saved the other half in case we needed help after we got on the ground." As the ARA ships banked away from the area, the four Huey gunships ran ahead of the troop carriers and blazed their machine guns into the wilderness, hoping to the keep the enemy's head down while the air cavalrymen prepared for their landing.

"As the chopper skids touched the ground I yelled, 'Let's go!' and jumped out running for the trees on the western edge of the clearing, firing my rifle." It was 10:48 a.m. on that Sunday morning when Hal Moore and the lead elements of Bravo Company touched down at LZ X-Ray.[139]

Just then, Crandall and his pilots lifted off and raced back to Plei Me, off to gather the next wave of troops. Moore continued running across the open clearing, firing his rifle into the brush. After he had gone about seventy-five yards, he paused briefly to insert a fresh magazine into his M-16. Looking up from the landing zone, he noticed that "the heavily forested slopes of the Chu Pong rose steep and dark more than a thousand feet above the clearing. The massif's lower slopes were covered with thick green foliage, elephant grass, and tangles of brush. Gullies and long fingers of ground led from the bottom of the mountain and blended into the woods and the dry creek bed where we stood. Plenty of spaces for people to hide. The creek bed just inside the western edge of our clearing was an excellent route of approach for enemy troops coming from the direction of the mountain or the valley, and for us going the other way. That creek bed was a critical feature."[140]

Suddenly, Moore realized that there was no enemy in sight. Yet that's exactly what worried him. "Nothing was wrong, except that nothing was wrong. I had a strong sense that we were under direct observation from the enemy." Moore was correct—high atop the Chu Pong massif, elements of the 66th and 33rd NVA Regiments lay waiting. Senior Lieutenant Colonel Nguyen Huu An later told Moore that "we had a very strong position and a strong mobile command group. We were ready, had prepared for you and expected you to come. The only question was when. The trees and brush limited our view of the helicopter landing but we had an observation post on top of the mountain and they reported to us when you dropped troops and when you moved them."

These regiments on the Chu Pong massif had been scheduled to participate in a November 16 attack on Plei Me. However, the arrival of Moore's battalion at X-Ray promptly changed the NVA's plans. "Plei Me would have to wait. The 66th and 33rd Regiments would attack the landing zone and destroy the Americans by noon," or so they hoped.[141]

Meanwhile, Moore sent Herren's 1st Platoon to reconnoiter the area west of the creek bed. "Herren had most of his troopers on the ground; the rest were on their way in the second lift." After only a few minutes into their reconnaissance, however, Sergeant Larry Gilreath found an enemy soldier wandering the area. Frightened, the young Vietnamese took off running but, after a short chase, one of the 1st Squad NCOs tackled him to the ground. "He wasn't much, but he was this battalion's first prisoner in Vietnam: about five feet seven inches tall, maybe twenty years old . . . wild eyed and trembling with fear." Claiming to be a deserter, the young man was unarmed, barefooted, and wore the unmistakable khaki uniform of a North Vietnamese regular.[142]

Troopers from Bravo Company, 2-7 Cavalry, stand up in the elephant grass to get a better view as they fire into pockets of North Vietnamese snipers outside the US perimeter at LZ X-Ray.
© *Associated Press*

Moore wasted no time. In the meat-grinder battles of Korea, he had learned to avoid lengthy interrogations. Through Mr. Nik's interpretations, Moore asked the young NVA "How many of you are there?" and "Where are they?" The prisoner's response was hardly encouraging. There were three battalions on the mountain, all of whom were anxious to kill Americans but as of yet could not find any. "Three battalions of enemy added up to more than 1,600 men against the 175-plus Americans currently on the ground here."[143]

Moore then told Herren to intensify his patrols and be prepared to assume Charlie Company's mission of exploring the foot of the Chu Pong. "If those enemy battalions were on their way, we needed to engage them as far off the landing zone as possible." Moore radioed Dillon to land the fire support chopper on the LZ and take the NVA deserter back to division headquarters for further questioning.[144]

Meanwhile, Tony Nadal and his men in Alpha Company arrived on the battlefield. The young Captain asked if he could follow Bravo Company into the woods, but Hal told him to stay and secure the LZ. By now, Herren had sent his three platoons northwest up the face of the Chu Pong massif. At 12:15 p.m., shots suddenly rang out from the area where the prisoner had been captured. Bravo Company was now in contact. "Even as the first shots rang out," Moore said, "I was radioing Herren to saddle up the rest of his Bravo Company men and move out fast toward the mountain to develop the situation." Hal knew he had to fight the enemy in the thick of the jungle. The dense foliage, combined with artillery and close air support, would be the only chance they had to survive a full-on enemy assault. If the enemy swarmed the LZ, the fight would be over.[145]

Responding to the gunfire, Herren ordered his 1st and 2nd Platoons to move out abreast of each other with 3rd Platoon following behind as a tactical reserve. 1st Platoon was led by Lieutenant Al Denvey, an eager but generally level-headed young officer. His counterpart in 2nd Platoon, Lieutenant Henry T. Herrick, however, was the polar opposite. Although Herrick was a gifted tactician, he was aggressive and bull-headed to the point of recklessness. Back at Fort Benning, Moore had briefly considered giving Herrick command of the Recon Platoon, a coveted job among infantry lieutenants. When Moore mentioned the idea to Sergeant Major Plumley, his response was shocking: "Colonel, if you put Lieutenant Herrick in there, he will get them all killed." Moore could hardly fathom how a new lieutenant could leave such a bad impression on the Sergeant Major that early.[146]

On one occasion, Herrick's own platoon sergeant, Sergeant First Class Carl Palmer, had confided to Captain Herren that the lieutenant's foolhardy aggressiveness might get the platoon killed. In fact, one of Herrick's men had drowned during a tactical river-crossing. According to the platoon sergeant, Herrick's heavy-handed aggression had been partly to blame. Although Herren couldn't prove that Herrick had been negligent, he couldn't fault the young lieutenant simply for being aggressive. Today, however, the sergeant's dreadful prophecy would come true.[147]

As the two platoons moved out to meet the enemy, Denvey's platoon moved ahead of Herrick's and at 12:45, 1st Platoon came under heavy fire from both flanks. Pinned down, Denvey appealed for help, at which point Herren radioed Herrick to reinforce 1st Platoon. However, on his way to Denvey's position, Herrick's platoon ran into a squad of North Vietnamese "moving towards X-Ray along a well-used trail, parallel to the platoon's direction of advance." Startled, the enemy squad retreated back up the hill. However, instead of continuing towards his beleaguered comrades in 1st Platoon, Herrick diverted his men to pursue the enemy squad. Sergeant Ernie Savage, one of Herrick's young NCOs, recalled that Herrick "made a bad decision, and we knew it was a bad decision. We were breaking contact with the rest of the company. We were supposed to come up on the flank of 1st Platoon; in fact we were moving away from them. We lost contact with everybody."[148]

Little did Herrick realize that he was leading his men into an ambush. Farther up the trail, Herrick's two lead squads came in contact with forty to fifty North Vietnamese who were rushing down the hill. During the first few minutes of the ensuing firefight, Herrick's platoon took no casualties; 3rd Squad's grenadiers kept the enemy at bay. But Herrick soon reported that the enemy was closing in on his flanks.

Herrick then realized that his platoon was in over their heads. As the enemy intensified their attack, and he began taking casualties, Herrick ordered his men to form a defensive perimeter on a nearby knoll. By this time, however, the platoon was no longer combat effective. Within half an hour of first contact, Lieutenant Herrick fell fatally wounded. Drawing his last breaths, he turned command of his platoon over to Sergeant Palmer and ordered his men to destroy the signal codes, lest they fall into enemy hands. Herrick's last known words were: "If I have to die, I'm glad to give my life for my country."

The situation atop the grassy knoll continued to deteriorate as Sergeant

American artillery at Firebase Falcon provide indirect fire support to the beleaguered troops at LZ X-Ray. © *Associated Press*

Palmer and Sergeant Robert Stokes—the next ranking NCO—were killed in action. This left twenty-one-year-old Sergeant Ernie Savage to control the fight. Scrambling to save his battered platoon from being overrun, Savage grabbed the radio and began calling artillery fire down on his position. By now, eight men in 2nd Platoon had been killed and another thirteen were critically wounded. As the news made its way back to Moore, he realized that "my worst case scenario had just come to pass: we were in heavy contact before all my battalion was on the ground. And now I had to deal with a cut-off platoon."[149]

The first wave of Charlie Company troops arrived at 1:32 p.m. "I had decided to commit Charlie Company toward the mountain," Moore said, "and take the risk of leaving my rear unguarded from the north and east." Moore grabbed Captain Bob Edwards, the Charlie Company commander, almost as soon as he dismounted his helicopter. Screaming over the gunfire, he ordered the young Captain to tie his men in with Alpha Company near the creek bed. The dry creek bed which ran through Alpha's sector was a vital terrain feature. As Moore had noted earlier, it gave the enemy an unhindered avenue of approach. Hal knew that the NVA would eventually try to outflank him—and he wanted to cut off their only clear path to the LZ. As Captain Edward's men

The battalion command group. Standing from left to right: Sergeant Major Plumley, S-3 Matt Dillon, Hal Moore, and Tom Metsker. Kneeling from left to right: an unidentified trooper and Bob Ouellette, the radioman. *Photo Courtesy of Joseph Galloway*

fell into position, Moore told Captain Nadal to tie into Herren's Bravo Company and to send a platoon to recover Lieutenant Herrick's men on the knoll.[150]

Around this time, Moore noticed that the "snaps and cracks of the rounds passing nearby took on a distinctively different sound, like a swarm of bees around our heads." This meant that the gunfire was getting closer and that the enemy was now shooting directly at him. Moore was in the middle of a radio transmission when Sergeant Major Plumley grabbed him by the shoulder. "Sir, if you don't find some cover, you're going to go down—and if you go down, we all go down!" He knew Plumley was right. After all, the Viet Cong and NVA were notorious for targeting officers. "The Sergeant Major pointed to a large termite hill . . . located in some trees in the waist between the two open areas of the landing zone." Although a good thirty yards away, Moore, Plumley, Metsker, and Mr. Nik made a run for it. Getting to the mound, however, was no easy task. For in those thirty yards, at least a dozen bullets kicked up the dirt around their feet as they ran for the cover of the termite mound. "That termite hill, the size of a large automobile, would become the battalion command post, the aid station, the supply point, the collection area for enemy prisoners, weapons, and equipment, and the place where our dead were brought."[151]

At 1:38 p.m., the next wave of soldiers from Alpha and Charlie Company landed at LZ X-Ray. By now, Moore had radioed to Matt Dillon to bring in airstrikes, and rocket-launching Hueys, along with the continuing artillery. With the enemy continuing to stream down the hill, Moore hoped that the relentless overhead fire would take the pressure off his ground troops.

Meanwhile, Alpha Company's 3rd Platoon, under Lieutenant Robert Taft, tore into the enemy at the creek bed. Expecting to meet Viet Cong guerrillas, they were genuinely surprised to see that these combatants were NVA regulars. Throughout the day, the fight for the creek bed took an incredible toll on 3rd Platoon. During the first assault, Lieutenant Taft and many of his lead troops were cut down by enemy fire. "Taft's platoon, now led by Korean War veteran Sergeant Lorenzo Nathan, stood firm and stopped the momentum of the attack." Shaken, but not defeated, the NVA shifted their attack leftward to try to flank Bravo Company. This move put the enemy directly in front of Alpha's 2nd Platoon, under Lieutenant Joe Marm, who had moved up to tie-in with Bravo Company's left flank. Seeing the enemy flood into their sector, Marm's men opened up with a blaze of machine gun fire, killing some eighty NVA at near point-blank range.[152]

The last elements of Charlie Company touched down at 2:30 p.m., along

Moore's troops recover one of their slain comrades at LZ X-Ray, November 15, 1965. *Photo by Peter Arnett.* © *Associated Press*

with the first wave of Delta Company, under Captain Ray Lefebvre. "Purely by chance, he and several of his Delta Company men had run toward a critical section of the perimeter, an uncovered gap on the left flank of Tony Nadal's embattled Alpha Company troops." Charlie Company, meanwhile, faced a renewed enemy assault of nearly 200 NVA. Knowing that his small-arms fire could only hold them off for so long, Captain Edwards called in an artillery strike on the enemy formation. It was a horrific sight as some of the Charlie Company soldiers could see the NVA burning to death from the shellbursts.[153]

Back on the knoll, with what remained of Herrick's lost platoon, Ernie Savage brought his own artillery down on an equally aggressive enemy. His bones rattled with every explosion as the 105mm rounds landed closer and closer, trying to beat back an enemy that seemed unfazed by their mounting casualties. Whether it was fanaticism or pure insanity, the NVA was determined to overrun this lost platoon. "It seemed like they didn't care how many of them were killed," Savage remembered. "Some of them were stumbling, walking right into us. Some had their guns slung and were charging barehanded."[154]

Meanwhile, on the Alpha-Delta line, another NVA attack made its way toward Specialist 4 Russell Adams, a machine gunner with Alpha Company. With his steady feed of ammo from assistant gunner Specialist 4 Bill Beck, Adams unleashed his M-60 against the hoard of enemy troops. However, in the midst of their firefight, Adams was hit and the M-60 jammed. "We were being assaulted and I could see the enemy twenty-five yards out," Beck recalled. "It's surprising how fast you think and act in a situation like that. Lying prone, I opened the feed cover, flipped the gun over and hit it on the ground. It jarred the shells loose. I flipped it right-side up, slapped the ammo belt back in, slammed the feed cover closed and began firing again."

During a lull in the enemy attack, Beck finally had a chance to check on Adams. Adams had taken a bullet to the head but, miraculously, was still alive. "Adams helmet lay in front of me," Beck said, but when he picked it up, a portion of Adams's brain fell out. "I was horrified! I screamed over and over for a medic and tried to tell Adams . . . that he'd be all right. I told him the choppers would get him out soon." Fortunately, the field medic, Donal J. "Doc" Nall carried Adams to the medevac site. Adams survived his wounds that day, but remained partially paralyzed for the rest of his life. Moore later credited Adams and Beck for halting an enemy advance which had tried to split the American lines along Alpha and Charlie Company sector. Years later, at an

Moore coordinating indirect fires on the radio. During the battle, Moore knew that his artillery and close air support would be the discriminator in deciding an outnumbered fight against the NVA. *US Army photo*

As the first day of the battle drags on, a resupply helicopter from the 229th Air Assault Battalion delivers another load of goods to Moore's beleaguered cavalrymen. *US Army photo*

1-7 Cavalry troopers take a break during a lull in the fighting at LZ X-Ray. November 15, 1965. *US Army photo*

Delivering more troops to the battle-field, a Huey is directed to land. November 15, 1965. *US Army photo*

Lieutenant Cyril "Rick" Rescorla in the photo which graced the cover of *We Were Soldiers Once . . . and Young.* Rescorla was a British immigrant who joined the United States Army after being inspired by the American GIs who were billeted in his hometown during WWII. Rescorla tragically perished in the attack on the World Trade Center on September 11, 2001. *Photo by Peter Arnett. ©Associated Press.*

One of Moore's troopers looks down the scope of an enemy AK-47 scavenged from a dead NVA soldier. *US Army photo*

American-Vietnamese goodwill reunion in Hanoi, an enemy commander revealed that Beck's machine gun had been the most casualty-producing, direct-fire weapon of the day.

Farther down the line, Delta Company had begun taking heavy casualties. Captain Lefebvre and one of his platoon leaders had been wounded and were hastened back to the medevac point. The medevac helicopters, however, had called off their mission. Apparently, they had decided that the enemy fire at X-Ray was too intense for their liking. With casualties piling up, Bruce Crandall and his Huey pilots took it upon themselves to ferry the wounded back to Plei Me. During this time, Tom Metsker, Moore's intelligence officer was fatally wounded while helping Ray Lefebvre onto the nearest Huey.

The last of the battalion arrived at X-Ray at 3:20 p.m. One of those helicopters delivered Lieutenant Larry Litton, who immediately assumed command of Delta Company. Under Litton's direction, the company mortars pounded into the NVA along the Alpha-Bravo lines. Meanwhile, Delta's recon platoon dug into the northern and eastern edges of the LZ, thereby securing a 360-degree perimeter around X-Ray.

With the rest of his battalion on the ground, Moore tapped Alpha and Bravo to make another push to Herrick's platoon. During a brief lull in the fight, "John Herren and Tony Nadal had pulled their men back to the dry creek bed . . . so they could begin their attack from there. The troopers came to their feet at 4:20 p.m. and moved out of the creek bed on the attack. They didn't get very far. There was an immediate and furious reaction from the North Vietnamese." Indeed, Alpha and Bravo started taking casualties almost immediately. Bravo's advance came under fire from an enemy machine gun nest. Lieutenant Marm at first tried to disable it with a M72 LAW but to no avail. "After failing to knock it out with a LAW rocket and a thrown grenade, he decided to deal with it directly. He charged through the fire, tossed a hand grenade behind the hill, and then cleaned up the survivors with his M-16 rifle."[155]

This second push to the lost platoon stalled after about seventy-five yards when the Alpha-Bravo team hit another standoff with the NVA. To make matters worse, the North Vietnamese were now firing on Alpha Company with an M-60 machine gun which they had taken from a dead gunner in Herrick's platoon. After nearly a half-hour standoff, Moore granted Herren and Nadal permission to withdraw back to the LZ. Nightfall was approaching; the lost platoon would have to wait until tomorrow.

Meanwhile, Joe Galloway had spent the entire afternoon trying to find a way into LZ X-Ray. Earlier he had lined up with some other troopers who were boarding a helicopter in one of the subsequent waves to X-Ray. But before the Huey took flight, a Major spotted Galloway in his non-regulation tan beret and removed him from the aircraft. Galloway then shifted to Firebase Falcon, where he saw Matt Dillon loading up the battalion's resupply helicopter. Joe grabbed him by the shoulder and said "Matt, I need to get in there." Dillon replied that he was going back to X-Ray after nightfall and couldn't take him along without Moore's approval.[156]

"Well, get him on the radio," Joe said impetuously.

With that, Dillon returned to the firebase command center and contacted Moore on the battalion's radio frequency. After telling Moore that the resupply helicopter would be airborne soon, Dillon added, "Oh, by the way, that reporter Galloway wants to come in, too." Moore replied: "If he's crazy enough to want to come in here, and you've got room, bring him along." A delightful Galloway jumped on the resupply chopper and sped towards LZ X-Ray.[157]

Back at 3rd Brigade's Field Headquarters, Colonel Brown ordered the 2nd Battalion, 7th Cavalry (2-7) to send its own Bravo Company to assist the beleaguered cavalrymen at X-Ray. "Three platoons of Bravo Company, 2nd Battalion were pulling guard duty around Colonel Tim Brown's 3rd Brigade headquarters . . . and were the closest at hand and the easiest to move when Brown cast about for reinforcements." Bravo Company, 2-7, under Captain Myron Didyruk, arrived at LZ X-Ray around 5:00 p.m. Moore sent two of Didyruk's platoons to fill in the gaps between 1-7's Bravo and Delta Company along the northeast perimeter. Meanwhile, Didyruk's 2nd Platoon reinforced Charlie Company near the south.[158]

The first day of the battle had taken a heavy toll on the Americans. By nightfall, the 450-man battalion had lost eighty-five men killed or wounded. As the sun disappeared over the horizon, Moore and his men dug in for the night. The fury of the enemy's daylight attack had died down, but he knew they would continue to probe the perimeter, looking for any gaps in the Americans' line.

"For almost eight hours I had been involved in the minute-to-minute direction of the battle," said Moore. "Now I wanted to personally walk the perimeter and check the preparations for what promised to be a tough night and another tough day tomorrow. Just before dark, Sergeant Major Plumley and I broke away from the command post and set out to check the perimeter,

talking with the troopers and getting a feel for the situation on the
ground. What concerned me the
most was the morale of the men,
how well the companies were tied
in, their defensive fire plans, and the
situation with ammunition and
water supplies." From what Moore
could gather, the men's morale was
high. Despite their losses, they had
stopped a ferocious and determined
enemy from breaking through their
lines. As Moore walked the perimeter, his troops greeted him with af-
firmations like: "We'll get 'em sir"
and "They won't get through us, sir."
He was proud to command such
gallant men. Every company had at
least fifteen to twenty men who
were two weeks or less from the end
of their enlistments. Some of these

Young UPI reporter Joe Galloway, August 1965.
Photo courtesy of Joseph Galloway

brave short-timers now lay dead. "The rest of them were on that perimeter,"
Moore said, "standing shoulder to shoulder with their buddies, ready to continue the fight."[159]

That night, Moore checked in, via radio, on the status of Herrick's lost
platoon. Ernie Savage radioed back that he had taken no additional casualties
and continued to stand his ground. "I mulled over possible options for their
rescue: a night attack; night infiltration to reinforce the platoon; or a fresh attempt to fight through to them early the next morning. They would be on all
our minds this night, that brave handful of men surrounded and alone in a
sea of enemies."

Thus ended the first night of the battle.

At 6:20 a.m., November 15, Moore sent his companies out on reconnaissance
patrols to probe for any NVA lingering near the perimeter. He knew that the
enemy had inched their way closer to the landing zone during the night. The
nighttime artillery would have disrupted their movements down the Chu

Pong massif, but Hal was certain that some of them had made it through.

Barely half an hour into the recon patrol, Moore's hunch once again proved correct—Charlie Company's 1st and 2nd Platoons made contact with the NVA about 150 yards from the perimeter. The resulting firefight sent both platoons reeling back into the perimeter. 2nd Platoon, under Lieutenant Jack Geoghegan, was hit particularly hard. Geoghegan, twenty-four, had joined the battalion in its early days at Fort Benning. He and his wife Barbara had just welcomed the birth of their daughter, Camille, three months before his departure to Vietnam. During 2nd Platoon's retreat to the perimeter, one of Geoghegan's soldiers, PFC Willie F. Godboldt, was hit while firing his rifle from a covered position. Hearing his soldier cry out in pain, Geoghegan leapt from his foxhole and attempted to rescue Godboldt from the enemy on-slaught. But when he reached Godboldt's position, the young lieutenant was shot in the back and in the head. He died instantly. PFC Godboldt, the man he was trying to save, succumbed to his wounds a few minutes later.

Charlie Company continued to hold the line for the next hour, but by 7:45 a.m., enemy fire had begun to penetrate the perimeter. With the LZ under attack from all three sides, Lieutenant Charlie Hastings, the battalion's USAF liaison officer and forward air controller, made a bold and decisive call. He scrambled for his radio and transmitted the words "Broken Arrow"—meaning that an American unit was in danger of being overrun and for all available attack aircraft to be diverted for close air support. "We had aircraft stacked at 1,000 foot intervals from 7,000 feet to 35,000 feet, each waiting to receive a target and deliver their ordnance."[160]

To direct the incoming ordnance, "all platoons threw colored smoke grenades to define our perimeter for the pilots." Minutes later, a pair of F-100 Super Sabre jets zoomed across the LZ. As Hal looked up, he saw them release their six-foot napalm canisters. Something, however, wasn't right—the planes appeared to be coming in too low and too fast. As Moore watched the napalm cans tumble overhead, he realized that they were headed straight for his dem-olition team, dug in to the right side of his command post. "I couldn't do any-thing about the first two napalm cans, but I had to do something to stop the pilot of the second plane, who was aimed directly at the left side of the com-mand post." If the pilot hit the bomb-release switch, his canisters would land directly on the battalion command post—taking out Moore, Galloway, Plum-ley, and the rest of the headquarters staff in a massive case of fratricide. Moore yelled to Hastings at the top of his lungs: "Call that son of a bitch off! *Call him off!*" Terrified, Hastings screamed into his radio: "Pull up! Pull up!"[161]

The second plane aborted its mission and banked off to the left. However it was too late for the first plane—its napalm cans had already been released. In an instant, Moore's demolition team found themselves engulfed in a fiery storm of napalm. Joe Galloway remembered: "Before, I had walked over and talked to the [combat] engineer guys in their little foxholes. Now those same men were dancing in the fire. Their hair burned off in an instant. Their clothes were incinerated. One was a mass of blisters; the other not quite so bad, but he had breathed fire into his lungs. When the flames died down we all ran into the burning grass. Somebody yelled at me to grab the feet of one of the charred soldiers. When I got them, the boots crumbled and the flesh came off and I could feel the bare bones of his ankles in the palms of my hands." Those who perished from the napalm included PFC Jimmy Naka-yama, a Japanese-American soldier whose wife had just given birth to their baby daughter back in the States.[162]

Meanwhile, Charlie Hastings stood in agony as he watched the tragic and

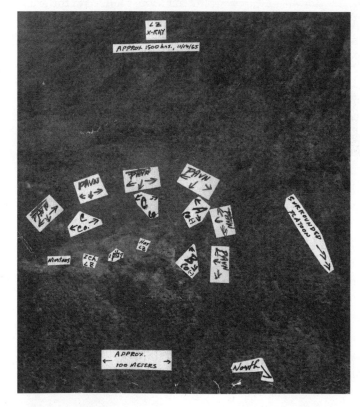

A photograph with Moore's hand-written notations depicting the situation at LZ X-Ray at approx-imately 3:00 p.m. on November 14, 1965. *The Hal Moore Collection*

Soldiers at LZ X-Ray evacuate one of their wounded, November 15, 1965. *Photo courtesy of Joseph Galloway*

unintended consequences of his airstrike. But Hal Moore looked at the grief-stricken lieutenant and told him: "Don't worry about that one, Charlie. Just keep them coming." Tragic as it was, Moore knew he couldn't let the miscalculated airstrike affect his young liaison officer. Air support was vital to keeping the NVA off the landing zone. One misplaced bombing run was no reason to lose their bearings in a life-or-death firefight.[163]

At 9:10 a.m., Alpha Company of 2-7 Cavalry, under Captain Joel Sugdinis, arrived at LZ X-Ray. Moore sent Sugdinis and his men to reinforce what remained of Charlie Company. Over the past twenty-four hours, Charlie Company had taken forty-two KIA and twenty wounded. One of Captain Didyruk's platoon leaders, Lieutenant Rick Rescorla recalled the horrific sight of Charlie Company's battered lines: "There were American and NVA bodies everywhere. My area was where Lieutenant Geoghegan's platoon had been. There were several dead NVA around his platoon command post. One dead trooper was locked in contact with a dead NVA, hands around the enemy's throat. There were two troopers—one black, one Hispanic—linked tight together. It looked like they had died trying to help each other."[164]

Despite the heavy toll taken on Charlie Company, the NVA had suffered much worse. With their own casualties on the rise, the NVA finally withdrew from Charlie Company's sector. "Although the enemy had withdrawn, he had left stay-behind snipers, and Didyruk's men came under sporadic fire, as did the landing zone and the battalion command post. The North Vietnamese had been beaten back but hadn't quit yet. Out in the Charlie Company sector, Sergeant Major Plumley and I walked through the horrible debris of battle. We found Lieutenant Jack Geoghegan's body; the two of us personally carried him from the battlefield."[165]

Meanwhile, 3rd Brigade sent another of its battalions, 2-5 Cavalry, under Lieutenant Colonel Bob Tully, to Moore's aid. Arriving at 12:05 p.m., Tully and Moore devised the following plan: "I would give him Captain John Herren's Bravo Company, 1st Battalion, which knew the ground and the route, and he would leave me his Bravo Company and his Delta Company. Tully would carry out a battalion-size assault, preceded by heavy fire support, with two companies abreast on line, and one company trailing in reserve." This formation would spearhead the final push to rescue Sergeant Savage and the lost platoon. The rescue force slowly made its way towards the lost platoon without enemy contact.

Once at the knoll, Tully's ad hoc relief force discovered just what a horrific fight Herrick's platoon had had. Of the twenty-nine men who had ventured into the NVA snare on November 14, nine were dead and thirteen were severely wounded. For two horrible nights, young Ernie Savage had mustered the strength to hold his platoon together as they endured one NVA probe after another. Now, he and the rest of 2nd Platoon rejoined their comrades on the line.[166]

A lone trooper stands over the bodies of his fallen comrades from Lieutenant Herrick's "Lost Platoon." Following Herrick's demise, Sergeant Ernie Savage held the platoon together for the remainder of the battle until their relief force arrived. November 16, 1965. *Photo by Rick Merron.* ©*Associated Press*

By the end of the day on November 15, the four companies in Moore's battalion "were down to a total of eight officers and 260 men. Charlie Company was no longer combat-effective as a rifle company. But we had a fresh battalion plus those two rifle companies from the 2nd Battalion, 7th Cavalry. With only light probes of the perimeter during the afternoon, the line companies had ample time to reorganize for the night ahead."[167]

The Americans received sporadic enemy fire throughout the night until 4:22 a.m. when the battered North Vietnamese tried one final assault on the American LZ. A force of nearly 300 NVA attacked Didyruk's Bravo Company. However, through a combination of judicious small arms fire and pinpoint artillery, Didyruk's men beat back the NVA onslaught. A lull in the fight followed until about 6:30 a.m. when the North Vietnamese caught their second wind. Once again, however, the enemy's desperate assault was cut down by American artillery. The few lucky dismounts who made it through the artillery soon fell under Bravo Company's rifle and machine gun fire.

By the late morning of November 16, the NVA had been attritted to the point where they were no longer combat effective. When the enemy quit the field early that morning, Hal Moore's battalion had been reinforced by 2/7 and 2/5 Cavalry and commanded superiority of indirect fires. "Now came the body count. From the beginning of the fight I had known that higher headquarters would eventually want to know what damage we had done to the enemy. With the battle raging back and forth over three days and two

Dead, poncho-covered bodies of Moore's young soldiers gives mute evidence of the horrific battle fought at LZ X-Ray, November 16, 1965. *Photo by Peter Arnett.* ©*Associated Press*

nights, it was anything but orderly. There was no referee to call time out for a body count. We did the best we could to keep a realistic count of enemy dead." In the end, Moore estimated 1,215 enemy soldiers killed. The Americans had lost 79 troops killed in action and 121 wounded.[168]

The battle had been the most devastating of Moore's life. He had seen his beloved troopers, the men whom he had commanded for eighteen months, many of them still in their teens, battle a ferocious enemy in the opening stages of a war that, as of yet, remained ill-defined and was plagued by a clumsy top-down management. He had seen many of his men perish under the most horrible conditions and he had carried several of his dead soldiers from the battlefield.

"But," as Moore admitted, "the body count on both sides, tragic as it was, did not go to the heart of the matter. What happened here in these three days was a sea change in the Vietnam War. For the first time since Dien Bien Phu, the North Vietnamese Army had taken the field in division strength. The People's Army soldiers were pouring down the Ho Chi Minh Trail in unprecedented numbers, and now they had intervened directly and powerfully on the battlefield in South Vietnam. The cost of America's involvement in this obscure police action had just risen dramatically."[169]

That afternoon, 2/7 and 2/5 Cavalry relieved Moore's battalion at LZ X-Ray."It was almost 3:00 p.m. and there were only a few of us left in the command post to load out," including Matt Dillon, Charlie Hastings, Sergeant Major Plumley, and Moore himself. He loaded himself on the final Huey and, true to his promise, Hal Moore was the last man of his unit to step off the battlefield.[170]

The following day, Moore's "sister battalion," 2/7 Cavalry departed X-Ray and began a tactical march to LZ Albany, a few miles to the northeast. However, Lieutenant Colonel McDade's men in 2-7 were savagely ambushed at Albany, which resulted in a near-massacre of the entire battalion. In total, 155 men were KIA/MIA with an additional 124 wounded.

On Tuesday, November 23, 1965, Moore relinquished command of 1st Battalion, 7th Cavalry to Lieutenant Colonel Raymond Kampe. "For the change of command, I requested a full battalion formation with officers front and center, the division band trooping the line, honors to the reviewing officer and the colors, and then the pass and review—reminiscent of our weekly Retreat parades back at Fort Benning."[171]

Moore also requested that the elements of 2/7 Cavalry who had fought alongside them at X-Ray be included in the ceremony. Specialist 4 Ray Tanner, of 1/7's Alpha Company remembered the raw emotions of that day: "We stood in formation, with some units hardly having enough men to form up. Colonel Hal Moore spoke to us and he cried. At that moment he could have led us back into the Ia Drang. We were soldiers, we were fighting men, and those of us who were left had the utmost love and respect for our colonel and for one another." That same day, General Kinnard promoted Moore to full Colonel. One month later, Moore assumed command of the division's 3rd Brigade.[172]

Meanwhile, in Washington and in Hanoi, political and military leaders pondered the implications of this explosive conflict in the Central Highlands of Vietnam. "Projections of the eventual cost in human lives and national resources, and even the eventual outcome, were promptly drawn for the American president, Lyndon Johnson, by his cool, number-crunching secretary of defense, Robert S. McNamara, and just as promptly set aside. This was America's war now, and America had never lost a war."[173]

Back in Hanoi, however, General Giap had a much more optimistic outlook. He determined that his troops had learned enough from the battle to defeat (or at least neutralize) the Americans' helicopter advantage. His troops had been devastated in the Ia Drang campaign, suffering a 12:1 kill-loss ratio in favor of the Americans. But these body counts were not what concerned him. He and Ho Chi Minh focused on something entirely different: "Their peasant soldiers had withstood the terrible high-tech fire storm delivered against them by a superpower and had at least fought the Americans to a draw. By their yardstick, a draw against such a powerful opponent was the equivalent of a victory. In time, they were certain, the patience and perseverance that had worn down the French colonialists would also wear down the Americans." Unfortunately, they were right.

A few days later, Moore briefed Secretary McNamara in An Khe and did his best to portray the harsh realities of the Ia Drang campaign. The NVA were no joke: they were well-trained, well-disciplined, possessed a sort of "suicidal fanaticism," and attacked the American lines with unflinching aggression.

As Moore continued his briefing, McNamara sat in furrowed silence. "He knew that the Vietnam War had just exploded into an open-ended and massive commitment of American men, money, and materiel to a cause that he

Moore uncovers the body of a dead NVA soldier near LZ X-Ray. Throughout the battle, Moore's battalion claimed the lives of over 1,200 enemy soldiers. *Photo by Peter Arnett*

was beginning to suspect would be difficult to win." On his way back to Washington, McNamara drafted a memo to President Johnson. Within its pages, he outlined two options: go for a diplomatic solution or rapidly increase the number of US forces in Vietnam. Accordingly, the US would have to send upwards of 600,000 troops if they expected to win. Still, McNamara warned that these deployments would not guarantee success, especially if Red China or the Soviet Union intervened. Plus, US casualties could reach as high as 1,000 per month by 1967. Nevertheless, Johnson and his advisors decided it was too late to turn back now. If the current kill-loss ratio stayed in favor of the Americans, the White House was certain they could bleed out the enemy within the next few years.[174]

Men like Moore and Kinnard, however, were less optimistic. "Those of us who had commanded American soldiers in the opening days had already undergone one crisis of confidence in the political leadership's commitment to the struggle," especially when President Johnson refused to extend enlistments and shipped US forces off to war terribly understrength. Now, in the wake of Ia Drang, Moore had even less confidence in his leaders' ability to prosecute the war.[175]

Worse, the North Vietnamese regiments in the Ia Drang had withdrawn into Cambodia. Moore and his troopers wanted to follow them, but were forbidden to do so under the rules of engagement. To Harry Kinnard, these rules were senseless and unproductive. "I was always taught as an officer that in a pursuit situation you continue to pursue until you either kill the enemy or he surrenders. I saw the Ia Drang as a definite pursuit situation and I wanted to keep after them. Not to follow them into Cambodia violated every principle of warfare. I was supported in this by both the military and civilian leaders in Saigon. But the decision was made, back there, at the White House, that we would not be permitted to pursue into Cambodia."[176]

Furthermore, Kinnard dismissed the notion that Giap and the North Vietnamese ever learned how to counter the US airmobile tactics. "What he learned," Kinnard said, "was that we were not going to be allowed to chase him across a mythical line in the dirt." That condition gave Giap all the advantage he needed. He could lure the Americans into battle at a time of his choosing and, when his troops got tired, they could flee into Cambodia where he knew they could regroup without any harassment from the Americans.[177]

With the conclusion of the Ia Drang campaign, the course had been set for America's combat mission in Vietnam.

Moore and Plumley at the Pleiku base camp following the Battle of Ia Drang. *The Hal Moore Collection*

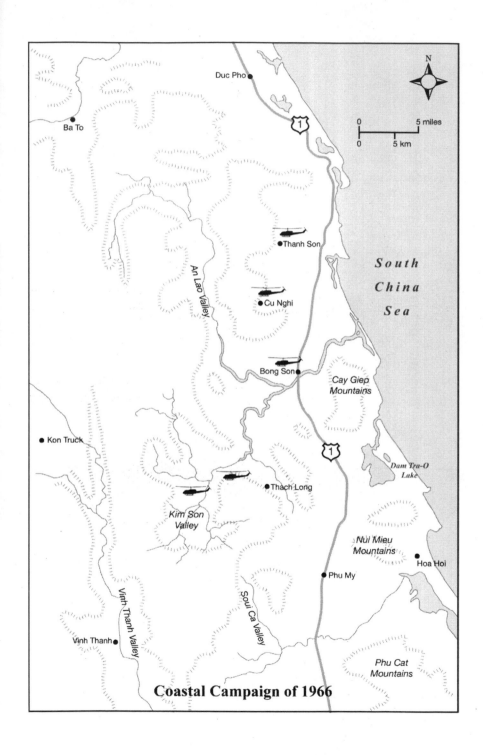

Coastal Campaign of 1966

CHAPTER SIX

THE COASTAL CAMPAIGN, 1966

Relinquishing command of 1/7 Cavalry was among the more bittersweet moments of Moore's career. For eighteen months, he had commanded, nurtured, and fought alongside the bravest men he had ever known. They shared a sacred bond which could be forged only in the fires of combat. In those eighteen months, he had become intimately familiar with the troopers and their families—remembering birthdays, anniversaries, and even children's names. But the time had come to take the next step. In December 1965, General Kinnard gave Hal Moore command of the 1st Cavalry Division's 3rd Brigade.

Secretary of Defense Robert McNamara and General William Westmoreland meet with troops in South Vietnam. Following the Battle of Ia Drang, McNamara and President Johnson decided to increase the American presence in Vietnam. *US Marine Corps photo*

Colonel Moore finding time to relax in Pleiku, December 1965. *The Hal Moore Collection*

By 1966, Allied progress against the Viet Cong and NVA had been slow, but encouraging. By the standards of attrition warfare, the Americans were well ahead in the game. Despite heavy losses, they had won a hard-earned victory at Ia Drang. Now, in the New Year, MACV cast its eyes toward the enemy stronghold in the coastal province of Binh Dinh. The goal was to break the Viet Cong's grip over the eastern part of the province, whose agricultural produce was vital to South Vietnam.

By attacking the enemy in Binh Dinh, the 1st Cavalry Division sought to envelop the Viet Cong and systematically destroy them through a series of aggressive helicopter assaults. Airmobility would mitigate the rough terrain and allow the 1st Cavalry troopers to strike at the enemy's base camps deep within the jungle valleys.[178]

Operation Masher marked the beginning of the coastal campaign—and Moore's 3rd Brigade would lead the charge. Beginning on January 25, 1966, Colonel Moore led his combat-tested brigade in an assault on the Viet Cong base near Bong Son. This operation pitted 3rd Brigade against the 2nd Viet Cong Regiment and the 7th and 9th Battalions of the 22nd NVA Regiment. "The operation began with 2-7 Cavalry moving to Bong Son," Moore said, "and clearing the area north, toward a proposed command post/forward support location, while 1-7 Cavalry made a diversionary move toward Chop Chai Hill." As 2-7 moved north on January 25 and 26, they made light enemy contact—mostly from NVA and Viet Cong mortar teams.[179]

In the first wave of the attack, Lieutenant Colonel McDade's 2-7 Cavalry touched down on the beach, four miles north of Bong Son. Ever since the opening stages of Ia Drang, McDade and his battalion had been having exceptionally bad luck. They had somewhat recovered from their near-massacre at LZ Albany, but had tragically lost forty-two men in a C-123 crash near An Khe before Operation Masher even started.

Departing Pleiku and the Ia Drang, 1-7 Cavalry boards for Bong Son. Photo by MB Alford.
The Hal Moore Collection

Departing
An Khe
base camp,
December
1965. *The
Hal Moore
Collection*

Moore (left)
with Captain
Greg "Matt"
Dillon (center)
and Lt. Col.
John Burney,
1966. *The
Hal Moore
Collection*

As McDade's helicopters settled into the LZ, they were met with violent machine gun fire from VC hidden amongst the palm groves. Desperate to avoid the small arms fire and deliver the troops without sacrificing a chopper, the Huey pilots broke formation and scattered the lead company (Charlie Company under the command of Captain John Fesmire) over a 1,000-yard beachfront near the village of Cu Nghi. The village was a well-known supply hub for the Viet Cong and, according to Moore's after-action report, the VC were prepared to defend it to the death. "As 2/7 Cavalry moved north, they encountered stiffer opposition. At least two companies were encountered in well prepared positions." Indeed, as Charlie Company strove to breakout from Cu Nghi, Alpha Company—which had landed a few miles south—found itself halted by heavy machine gun fire. Alpha Company was trying to reach Fesmire's men at the village, but the Viet Cong had put up a wall of fire between the two companies.[180]

Meanwhile, Moore's old battalion, 1/7 Cavalry, touched down at LZ Papa, several miles west of Cu Nghi. Stepping off their helicopters, 1/7 quickly came under fire from the 9th Battalion, 22nd NVA Regiment. 1/7's advance to the Cu Nghi, however, was delayed when Bravo Company had to secure the crash site of a downed C-47 Chinook helicopter. As it were, the Chinook had been carrying a 105 mm howitzer and the Viet Cong, anxious to get their hands on an American artillery piece, fought an intense firefight with Bravo Company for control of it. The Americans finally won the fight for the crash site by leveling the howitzer's gun tube and firing it directly into the advancing Viet Cong.[181]

Back at Cu Nghi, Alpha Company had finally broken through the VC's outer defense and reached Charlie Company at the village proper. As day turned to night, McDade consolidated the two companies at Cu Nghi and brought in Bravo Company under the cover of artillery fire. At daybreak, he called in an airstrike to napalm the enemy defenses. Artillery continued to hammer the retreating Viet Cong and NVA, while Moore arrived on the scene with 2nd Battalion, 12th Cavalry. Farther north, Kampe's 1-7 Cavalry air assaulted into a series of blocking positions to cut off the enemy retreat.

"As both Cavalry battalions [2-7 and 2-12] moved north, they pursued remnants of the 7th PAVN, Quyet Tam [22nd NVA] Regiment. Meanwhile, 1/7 Cavalry still had contact with 3 platoons of NVA troops," who were trying to escape. In his after-action report, Hal indicated that 1-7 Cavalry continued receiving enemy contact through January 31. With the enemy fleeing from

Hal Moore confers with Major General Jack Norton, Commanding General of the 1st Cavalry Division, at Dong Tre Special Forces Camp, June 1966. *The Hal Moore Collection*

the "hammer" of 2-7 and 2-12 Cavalry, and running into the "anvil" of 1-7 Cav, "the VC forces broke into small bands and began a withdrawal to the north, northwest, and west." Their escape route took them into the depths of the An Lao Valley.[182]

As the enemy quit the fight at Cu Nghi, "sixteen enemy weapons were collected on the battlefield, and many documents provided intelligence information pertinent to the [22nd NVA] Regiment. One letter from a company commander to his battalion commander stated, 'The men are defecting . . . we are surrounded by ARVN and US troops . . . request permission to consolidate and attack tomorrow.' Evidently, the commander didn't give the subordinate leader such permission, for the rout continued on 31 January and 1 February."

The opening days of Operation Masher had cost the enemy 660 KIA and another 357 wounded. The Americans lost 121 men. But as the NVA and Viet Cong withdrew into the An Lao Valley, Hal Moore prepared to follow.[183]

On February 4, 1966, Moore readied the brigade for pursuit operations just as Colonel William Lynch's 2nd Brigade joined the fight. That same day, Operation Masher was renamed Operation Whitewing, as President Johnson protested that "Masher" sounded too harsh and didn't reflect a "pacification emphasis." Political semantics aside, however, the enemy was still on the run, and the Airmobile Division was right on their heels.[184]

Now that 2nd Brigade had been committed to the fight, General Kinnard reassigned Moore's brigade farther south to the Kim Son Valley. Much like An Lao, Kim Son was a hotbed of Viet Cong activity and the local populace was decidedly pro-VC. For the Kim Son phase of the operation, Moore adjusted his tactics and tempo. He sent out "deceptive landings and other flight patterns to confuse enemy scouts." Moore indicated that he gave his battalions interlocking sectors "in which they were to establish ambush positions across the most likely avenues of egress from the area; this formed a circle of ambush positions around the operational area."[185]

Meanwhile, he placed company-sized elements atop hills overlooking key routes in and out of the valley. On February 11, 1966, these company combat teams displaced from their hilltops and descended into the VC camps, preceded by a hail of artillery fire. Taken together, the American advance and the artillery strike forced the enemy out from the center of the valley and straight into the ambush sites. At the end of the operation in Kim Son, "The 290 enemy body count compared to the 7 US KIAs," Hal wrote, "gave the US forces a kill ratio of over 40 to 1."

Returning to his command post at Bong Son on the morning of February 13, Moore's battle staff greeted him with a birthday cake and a thundering chorus of "Happy Birthday." He had been so intently focused on Whitewing that he had nearly forgotten today was his birthday. Touched and exuberantly grateful, Hal Moore broke out a bottle of Jim Bean bourbon (one of the few libations afforded to a brigade commander in combat) and proposed a toast: first to the President, then to

For his audacious leadership and courage under fire during the Battle of Ia Drang, Hal Moore receives the Distinguished Service Cross—the nation's second highest award for valor. *The Hal Moore Collection* victory in Vietnam, and finally to "the loyal, brave, and great infantry soldier who has run around tired, stinking, dirty, with wet feet under enemy fire. God Bless him."[186]

By mid-February, the 3rd Brigade rotated off the line and its operational areas were taken over by Colonel Roberts' 1st Brigade. Operation Masher/Whitewing ended on March 8, 1966. The enemy lost 1,342 soldiers in total, while Moore lost 228 of his own.[187]

Yet, even in the deadliest of battles, Moore always led from the front. A sergeant in one of Moore's battalions recalled that, during a short halt in a Bong Son cemetery, Moore saw a gleam of light from within a cluster of nearby trees—the reflection of a sniper's gun sight. Moore tackled the young sergeant to the ground just before the sniper's bullet ricocheted off a nearby gravestone. Two more shots followed before Hal rose to his feet and said, "Okay guys, let's get 'em." Leading a charge with only his sidearm pistol in hand, Hal sprinted from one gravestone to the next, shooting and hollering as his men followed close behind. By the end of the skirmish, twenty-two Viet Cong lay dead, eleven captured, and only one American was seriously wounded. Around this time, Hal's troops began calling him "One More Moore," as he always seemed to have one more fight in him.

On another occasion, Moore was travelling with the lead element of a patrol when he came across some of his troops attempting to throw a hand grenade into a bunker at the edge of a nearby village. Realizing that this operation was taking place near a populated area, Moore feared that there may have been women and children hiding in the bunker complex. He therefore

Moore and his troops during Operation Masher in Bong Son, January 1966. *Photo by Art Zich*

instructed his men to use a smoke grenade instead. Drawing from his experience in Occupied Japan, Moore remembered that one of his fellow officers had playfully thrown a smoke grenade into the Bachelor Officer Quarters at Camp Crawford. And, just as it had done in Japan, this smoke grenade cleared out the bunker within a matter of seconds. True to his hunch, a frightened posse of Vietnamese women and children emerged from the bunker—screaming and coughing, but otherwise unharmed. Although the smoke grenade was a heavy-handed tactic, Moore knew that it was better to positively identify the occupants of a bunker before engaging it with deadly fire.

"One More Moore" got another chance to pursue the Viet Cong in May 1966 when his 3rd Brigade comprised the main effort for Operation Davy Crockett. Beginning on May 4, Moore returned to the Bong Son plains to intercept two reported NVA battalions. "Since 2-7 Cavalry was blocking in the north and 1-7 Cavalry blocking in the west, with the ARVN to the east, it appeared that 1-9 Cavalry pushing north would trap the battalions [near the coastal village] by sundown."[188]

1-9 Cavalry led the air assault into Bon Song, and although the other battalions established their blocking positions, the retreating enemy managed to escape. Contact was re-established, however, on May 6 near the village of Thang Son. Determined not to let the VC get away again, Moore sent 2-7 south of the village to seal off any escape routes while 1-7 assaulted the village from the north. Caught within the pincer-like movement, the VC dug into their trench lines and prepared for a final stand at Thang Son. As both of Moore's battalions closed in on the VC, they called in an airstrike of twelve F4 Phantoms to strafe the village. The Air Force fighter-bombers delivered their bombs with such pinpoint accuracy that Moore said it was "the most accurate display of tactical air precision bombing I have ever seen." Moore's troops overran the VC battalion the following day.[189]

After the battle at Than Son, the 3rd Brigade once again searched the Kim Son Valley, but met only limited contact. Operation Davy Crockett ended nearly two weeks later on May 16, 1966. Total enemy casualties were 438 KIA; friendly casualties were only 27.

"After the May operation," Moore wrote, "it was clear to me, a battlefield commander not included in the politics of it all, that [MACV] had not succeeded in coordinating American and South Vietnamese military operations with follow-up Vietnamese government programs to re-establish control in

Colonel Hal Moore, 3rd Brigade Commander, at Bong Son in the days of Operation Masher. *Photo by Bob Poos.* ©*Associated Press*

Two 1st Cavalry Division soldiers drag a Viet Cong guerrilla from a bunker near a village in Bong Son during Operation Masher. January 29, 1966. *Photo by Kyoichi Sawada.* ©*Associated Press*

Colonel Moore (center) stands with Captain Dick Sundt, the 3rd Brigade Fire Support Officer,
and Captain Dick Merchant, Moore's Assistant S-3. Dinh Binh Province, April 1966.
The Hal Moore Collection

the newly cleared areas." This allowed the Viet Cong and NVA to retake large swaths of land from which they had previously been ousted. It was around this time that Hal began to realize the futility of this war. "If they couldn't make it work in Bong Son—where the most powerful American division available had cleared enemy forces from the countryside—how could they possibly hope to re-establish South Vietnamese control in other contested regions where the American military presence was much weaker? But it was 1966, and early in the war. All I could do was hope and pray that our terrible sacrifices would eventually contribute to the achievement of America's objectives in Vietnam."[190]

Those objectives, however, were unclear even to America's leadership. And the perennially poor decisions coming out of the Johnson White House only compounded the problem. In 1966, for example, Johnson announced that the standard tour of duty for all troops in Vietnam would be twelve months (except the Marines who were given thirteen month rotations). Under this policy, "those who had survived and learned to fight in this difficult environment began going home in the summer of 1966; with them went all their experience and expertise. Replacing them was an Army of new draftees, which in due course would be replaced by newer draftees. The level of training would drift ever lower as the demand for bodies grew."[191]

What frustrated Hal even more were the six-month term limits for battalion and brigade commanders. "This was ticket-punching," as he called it. Senior officers needed troop command assignments for promotion, but the accelerated timeline meant that the commander would be rotating out just as he was learning the tricks of the trade in Vietnam.

"In late June 1966, my turn was up as commander of 3rd Brigade. When my replacement, a Colonel straight out of the Pentagon, showed up to take over, my brigade was in the field, fighting near Dong Tre. It would have been criminal, in those circumstances, to relinquish command to a man who was still pissing Stateside water, and I flatly refused to do so." The change of command was therefore delayed until July 8, 1966—after the fighting was over.[192]

As it turned out, leading the 3rd Brigade was One More Moore's last hurrah in Vietnam. He departed from Saigon less than a week after his change of command. "I had hoped that my next assignment would be to the Infantry School at Fort Benning, where I could pass along what I had learned in Vietnam to the young officers who were headed for combat. It was not to be." In fact, of the hundreds of officers who had gone through airmobile training with the 11th Air Assault/1st Cavalry Division, only one returned to teach at the Infantry School. Moore, meanwhile, found himself in the queue for yet another assignment in Washington, DC.[193]

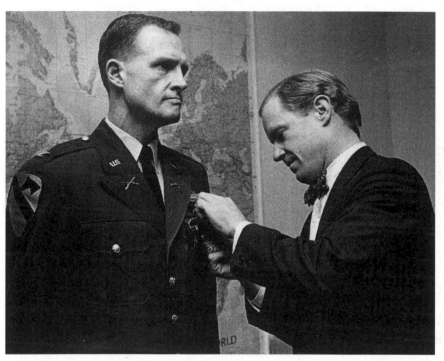

Moore receives the Joint Service Commendation Medal during an awards ceremony at the Pentagon, 1966. *The Hal Moore Collection*

CHAPTER SEVEN

COMMAND DECISIONS

J ust as she had done during the Korean War, Julie held the family together in her husband's absence. The Vietnam-era home front, however, had been particularly rough on her. Contrary to what the film *We Were Soldiers* portrayed, Julie and her fellow Army wives did not stay in their on-post quarters while their husbands were overseas. Instead, under one of the most dubious Army policies of the day, the wives of the 1st Battalion, 7th Cavalry were given 30 days to vacate their houses and move off-post until their husbands returned.

Some of the younger wives returned home to live with their families, "much as Julie had done during the Korean War," Hal said. But most of the officers' and senior non-commissioned officers' wives "scattered in a desperate search for housing in Columbus, Georgia, just outside the gates of Fort Benning." Most of them ended up in trailer homes or other low-rent housing areas. Julie found a small, three-bedroom home on the outskirts of Columbus and had the unenviable task of cramming her five children into the tiny dwelling. "Each night," Hal said, "she unfolded a cot for our son David, as there wasn't room for one more bed anywhere."[194]

But Julie's biggest challenge during this period had nothing do with the housing situation. On November 18, 1965, the first casualty telegrams from Vietnam arrived in Columbus, Georgia. Prefaced by the words, "The Secretary of the Army regrets to inform you," these telegrams were an Army spouse's worst nightmare. At best, the telegram would report its subject as "Missing in Action," giving some fearful Army wife a glimmer of hope that her husband was still alive. Normally, however, it brought the devastating news that her husband had been killed in action. But at this point, the war

Top photos: Moore is reunited with his family in Columbus, Georgia, 1966. After spending a year in Vietnam, he was glad to be home with his loved ones again. *The Hal Moore Collection*

was so new that the Army "had not even considered establishing the casualty notification teams." Instead, "Western Union simply handed the telegrams over to Yellow Cab drivers."[195]

The cab drivers were well aware of what these telegrams said, and many of them hated the delivery duty. Some drivers would calmly place the telegram in the recipient's hand and, without a single word, walk solemnly back to their taxi as the new widow broke down in tears on her front porch. Others would simply ring the doorbell, hastily shove the telegrams in the doorframe, and scurry back to their cabs hoping to avoid the unpleasant encounter. Julie remembered that these were the days when "the mere sight of a Yellow Cab cruising through the neighborhoods struck panic in the hearts of the wives and children of soldiers serving in Vietnam." Furious over the Army's lack of planning, and its cavalier attitude toward the Yellow Cab approach, Julie decided to take action.[196]

At first, she followed the cabs to their destinations trying to comfort the grief-stricken widows. Being the battalion commander's wife, Julie wasn't sure how she might be received. Privately, she feared that the new widows would take out their frustration on her—seeing Julie as a representation of the man who ordered their husbands into battle. Her fears, however, were unfounded as these wives were happy just to have someone nearby who cared.[197]

After relinquishing command of 3rd Brigade, Hal departed for the Office of

the Under Secretary of Defense where he spent the next year as the Military Liaison to the Assistant Secretary for International Affairs. As Moore described it, the job was a mind-numbing, bureaucratic post. His primary duties as the Military Liaison were to create "Trip Books" for senior Defense and State Department officials visiting Vietnam, and draft replies to what he called "Congressionals," or "letters [about] Vietnam from constituents of Senators and Congressmen."[198]

From these letters, it seemed that the country was growing more restless over the war in Vietnam. Even Moore himself had grave concerns. He had never warmed up to the Johnson-McNamara way of war and he hadn't forgotten the disastrous personnel policies which had stripped his battalion of its most experienced men on the eve of their deployment. Still, throughout 1967, it appeared as though Allied forces were making strides against the Communists. That year, "some two-thirds of the hamlets were judged secure and under the control of the central government," and US forces had killed nearly 81,000 Viet Cong and NVA. If these trends continued, General Westmoreland predicted that an orderly withdrawal could begin as early as 1970. However, in January 1968, the Tet Offensive drastically changed the course of American intervention in Vietnam.[199]

By the fall of 1967, Hanoi realized that the NVA stood no chance of defeating US forces in open combat. The Communists, therefore, settled on a different approach: if they couldn't defeat the Americans on the battlefield, then they could certainly disrupt their cheerful narrative of "rural pacifica-tion" and bring the US to the negotiating table. Under the cover of a "cease-fire" during Tet (the Vietnamese New Year), Hanoi directed the Viet Cong, supported by select NVA units, to launch a massive, simultaneous attack on several key US and ARVN installations, as well as urban centers and provin-cial capitals throughout the country. It was a bold move and, in truth, Hanoi wasn't entirely certain that it would succeed. But if it stood any chance to undermine South Vietnam's credibility and shake American confidence in its war effort, it was worth the risk.

Although the US and South Vietnamese forces effectively crushed the Viet Cong uprising, the American media painted a *very* different picture of the Tet Offensive. Television broadcasts showed frightening images of the Viet Cong storming the American Embassy in Saigon and the bloody fighting in Hue and Khe Sanh. Taken together, these haunting images led Walter Cronkite, America's most trusted news anchor, to declare that the war was now unwinnable. All at once, Johnson and McNamara lost their credibility as public opinion turned savagely against the war. Scrambling to save the administration's dignity, Johnson announced on March 31, 1968, that he would not seek re-election and would instead devote his attention to ending the war in Vietnam. Although Tet proved to be a resounding failure for the North Vietnamese, it gave the Hanoi bureaucrats exactly what they wanted— a crisis of confidence in the American war effort.

Amidst this public backlash, Moore also noticed that the American people

Moore (standing in the third row above the woman in the light full-length dress) with his fellow Master's students in the International Affairs degree program at Harvard University. Moore attended Harvard from 1967–68 as part of the Army's ongoing initiative to send its senior officers to obtain Master's degrees from Ivy League schools. *The Hal Moore Collection*

were growing increasingly hostile toward the military. Indeed, the soldiers who went to Vietnam with the Class of 1965 returned home to a very different society then the one they had left. The inspired patriotism of John F. Kennedy's "New Frontier" had disappeared in the social unrest and political turbulence of a "Great Society" which hardly lived up to its name. Even worse, many Americans were blaming the military simply for its involvement in the war. Moore could hardly believe it—US servicemen who had once been heralded as "heroes" were now being protested, spat upon, and called "baby killers."

None of this, however, dissuaded Moore from continuing his service. After earning his Master's Degree in International Affairs from Harvard, he reported yet again to the Pentagon, where he worked for the Deputy Chief of Staff for Operations (DCSOPS). At DCSOPS, Moore was at the forefront of implementing the US drawdown in Vietnam. By now, Johnson's turnabout on Vietnam had morphed into President Nixon's policy of "Vietnamization"— a redeployment of American combat forces while training the South Vietnamese to take the lead in combat operations. Vietnamization was essentially a three-step process: increase the ARVN's combat and logistical capabilities, systematically return the Corps Tactical Zones to Vietnamese control, and withdraw American ground forces.

Within the first few months of Hal Moore's tour at DCSOPS, he helped draft the Army's plan for withdrawing two brigades of the 9th Infantry Division from the II and III Corps' area south of Saigon. But as these two brigades made their way back across the Pacific, Hal received new orders to Korea in

Moore (seated at the far right, with legs crossed) participates in a foreign policy discussion with his fellow students at Harvard University. Moore graduated from Harvard in 1968 with a Master's degree in International Affairs. *The Hal Moore Collection*

Moore is promoted to Brigadier General on August 31, 1968 in a ceremony held
at the Pentagon. Moore receives his first stars from Lieutenant General Harry J. Lemley
and wife Julie while their children look on. Moore was the first member of his West
Point class to be promoted to one-star, two-star, and three-star general.
The Hal Moore Collection

July 1969. Reporting to General Charles H. Bonesteel, the commander of the
United States Forces Korea (USFK), Moore became "the Plans and Operations
Officer (G-3) of the Eighth Army in Korea. I was a brigadier general on the
two-star list." Moore recalled that his new office was located at Eighth Army
Headquarters in Seoul and that "I visited with military units on the front lines
of the Demilitarized Zone to check on the defense plans and to get to know
the terrain, roads, and the principal commanders." But as Moore soon found
out, the Republic of Korea wasn't the best place to be in 1969.[200]

In the summer of 1969, the DMZ was one of two frontiers in America's Cold
War—the other being the inter-German Border, the largest swath of the "Iron
Curtain." Like their comrades in East Germany, the North Koreans stood
across an impenetrable chasm of landmines and barbed wire fences, staring

down the Americans in passive anticipation of another conflict. The North Korean, however, was a different brand of Communist than his Eastern Bloc counterparts. Words like "Mutual Assured Destruction" and "Balance of Power" meant nothing to him. He pitied the South Korean capitalists and genuinely despised the Americans. His only concern was the reunification of Korea under Pyongyang's rule.

Sixteen years earlier, the Korean War had ended in a cease-fire. Thus, the two Koreas were, technically, still at war. And in recent years, the North Koreans had grown more audacious in testing the boundaries of the 1953 armistice. Occurring roughly between 1966 and 1969, they launched a series of low-level border incursion in what became known, unofficially, as the "Second Korean War." By the time Moore arrived in Korea, these border clashes had claimed the lives of over 40 American troops and nearly 400 North Koreans. On October 1, 1969, General Bonesteel relinquished his command of USFK to General John H. Michaelis, who had been the Commandant at West Point when Moore was an Infantry Tactics Instructor. Michaelis, in turn, negotiated the release of three US soldiers from an OH-23 helicopter which had been shot down north of the DMZ two months earlier. Their release on December 3, 1969 is generally regarded as the end of the "Second Korean War," but tensions remained at an all-time high and border incursions continued sporadically over the next quarter-century.

However, to Hal Moore, it seemed that the North Koreans were the least of the Eighth Army's worries. "During the latter Vietnam War years of 1969–1971," he said, "Korea was a hotbed of racial tensions and heavy drug use. These were the days of . . . marijuana, all colors of pills, and a lot of Koreans made their living selling these pills and marijuana to American soldiers. Altercations between black and white soldiers were frequent."[201]

Suddenly, the racial tensions in Korea exploded late one night in May 1970. On that night, Moore said, "the 7th Division [headquartered at Camp Casey along the DMZ] experienced a number of fights between black soldiers, white soldiers, and Hispanic soldiers. It was a major brawl that lasted all night." Shortly after midnight, Moore was awakened by his staff duty officer with an alarming report that the barracks had been trashed and several buildings were on fire, "including," Moore said, "the Post Library." It was a horrific sight: soldiers were being knifed and thrown out of second-story windows. Things were getting so out of control that the MPs had to call on the local Korean police for assistance.[202]

Camp Casey, South Korea, 1969. Camp Casey was headquarters for the 7th Infantry Division. During the latter years of the Vietnam War, Korea was a hotbed of racial tension among the Black, White, and Hispanic GIs. *Photo courtesy of Bruce Richards*

The entrance to Camp Casey, bearing Moore's name as the Commanding General and his "right hand man," Command Sergeant Major Don Peroddy. Moore and Peroddy went to great lengths to correct the racial problems and rampant drug use throughout the division. *Photo courtesy of Bruce Richards*

The main street of Dongducheon, outside the gates of Camp Casey. Dongducheon had several *bars*, brothels, and drug houses which were frequented by American soldiers. *Photo courtesy of Bruce Richards*

Moore was promoted to Major General shortly after taking command of the 7th Infantry Division. Pinning Moore's stars are General Michaelis and daughter Julie while Cecile and David look on. *The Hal Moore Collection*

Moore gathers with the children of Yang Ju Child Care Center, July 15, 1970. Moore's Division sponsored the Child Care Center as part of a public relations program to build better ties with the community. During his command tenure, 7th Division soldiers were a regular sight at Yang Ju—reading stories to and playing games with the children. *The Hal Moore Collection*

Left: Julie volunteers as a "candy striper" for the Red Cross Blood Drive at Camp Casey, June 1970. Throughout her husband's career, Julie was a tireless volunteer for many on-post functions and organized family readiness groups to promote camaraderie among her fellow Army spouses. *The Hal Moore Collection*

Center: The main entrance to Fort Ord, California during the early 1970s. Upon Hal Moore's return to the United States, he became the Commanding General of Fort Ord and the Army Training Center. *US Army photo*

Moore's assumption of command ceremony at Fort Ord, 1971. *The Hal Moore Collection*

Moore hosts Brigadier General Ana Mae Hays during a visit to Camp Casey, fall 1970. Hays was the Chief of the Army Nurse Corps and was the first woman in American history to wear the stars of a general officer. *The Hal Moore Collection*

Moore's home at the Presidio of Monterey, near Fort Ord. *The Hal Moore Collection*

Moore giving blood at the Camp Casey Blood Drive, June 1970. *The Hal Moore Collection*

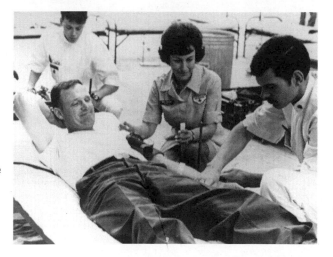

Meanwhile, Moore leapt out of bed and raced to his office. Although it was nearly 2:00 a.m., the entire Eighth Army Headquarters was swarming with staff officers—all frantically taking calls and rifling through various reports trying to get a hand on the situation at the DMZ. "Not long after that," Hal said, "my intercom squawked," where a voice on the other end said "General Michaelis wants to see you immediately."[203]

Michaelis wasted no time. "Moore, I've gotten permission from Washington to frock you with your second star," meaning that Moore would become a two-star general with the pay of a one-star until his official promotion date. General Michaelis had just relieved the 7th Division commander and now gave Moore simple instructions: "I want you to get up there and straighten out that goddamned division!"

"Yes sir," Moore replied. "When do I leave?"

"In half an hour."[204]

"The 7th Infantry Division was a typical division," Hal said, "draftees mostly." He felt a special connection to the unit, having served as a Regimental S-3 and company commander with the division during some of the bloodiest battles in the Korean War. Now, the division consisted of some 16,000 men and officers scattered across twenty-three camps in South Korea. Outside the Division Headquarters at Camp Casey was the village of Dongduchon, a modern-day Gomorrah where American GIs frequented its bars, drug houses, and brothels.[205]

"I went up there," Moore continued, "and I turned into a red-assed son of a bitch!" Almost immediately, he relieved a number of officers who were deemed incompetent.[206]

However, he was careful not to lump everyone into the same category. His new program of discipline was exactly what the unit needed, but he knew that if he treated the entire division like a gang of ruffians, it would backfire on him. "A leader should never tell an outfit that it's screwed up," Moore said. "If he does, then it will be screwed up. Why? Because the boss said so." A unit's performance and morale often reflects the attitude of its leadership. In the case of 7th ID, Moore knew that the unit was well aware of its deficiencies. Bludgeoning them with lectures would not earn their respect or their confidence. He instead decided to find out what things the division did well and what it needed to improve. This approach, along with a discussion of his "policies, standards, and goals," would be the first step to re-establishing order within the division.[207]

Over the next ten days, he flew his helicopter to each of the division's camps "and talked for fifteen minutes or so to every unit. Early on, it was clear to me that many of the race relations problems, and perceptions and real cases of discrimination, occurred at the small unit level. As I checked into that, the other small-unit leadership deficiencies came to light." To correct these problems at the small-unit level, Moore instituted an Officer's Leadership School for company-grade officers and an NCO Leadership School for staff sergeants and below. Each course was a week long and taught by instructors carefully selected from across the division. "These schools went a long way toward reducing the racial and drug abuse problems."[208]

Treating others with respect, fairness, and dignity was the next step to making his program successful. Unfair discrimination had led to many of the racial problems within the Army. Determined to solve the problem at its roots, Moore issued his Equal Opportunity Policy:

> People are our most important asset in the 7th Infantry Division. In all that we do, each person must be recognized as an individual; recognizing his aspirations, capabilities, and personal needs. Each man must be continually provided fair treatment and equal opportunity, within appropriate regulations, to rise to as high a level of responsibility as his talent and diligence will take him.[209]

He knew he couldn't change racial attitudes on his own, but he *could* make it a punishable offense for a leader to discriminate based on race, ethnicity, or creed.

Moore also understood that recreational and community service programs helped keep soldiers out of trouble. "I set up a lot of different athletic programs," Hal said. "We won the Eighth Army football championship, the boxing championship, and the basketball championship." After all, it was better for soldiers to "blow off steam" in the sports arena than in the streets of Dongduchon. Reaching out to the local community, Moore had the division sponsor the nearby Yang Ju Child Care Center. For the remainder of his command, 7th Division soldiers were a regular sight among the children; playing games with them, giving out food, and even teaching English.[210]

During this revitalization of 7th ID, Moore's ace in the hole came in the form of another rough-and-tumble Sergeant Major. Command Sergeant Major Don Peroddy was, in Moore's words, another "red-assed son of a bitch."

Hal Moore taking questions from the local press corps regarding the evolution of Project VOLAR (Volunteer Army). As the Army prepared for the end of the draft, VOLAR tested several programs to make Army life more appealing to a generation of volunteers. *The Hal Moore Collection*

Peroddy had done three combat tours in Vietnam for which he had earned multiple Purple Hearts and Silver Stars. Peroddy "straightened things out fast and kept them straight by putting NCOs in the bars and on the streets working with the military police. Early every morning and late every afternoon, I met with each of these men and we talked about immediate problems, developing situations, and whatever they or I wanted to bring up." Moore commanded the division until May 1971, when the unit cased its colors and turned its facilities over to the 2nd Infantry Division.[211]

Departing Korea, Moore took on a new assignment as the Post Commander and Commandant of the Army Training Center in Fort Ord, California. Nestled at the edge of Monterey Bay, and within driving distance of San Francisco, Fort Ord was one of the most sought-after assignments in the US military. It was the main hub of the Fort Ord Military Complex which included the Presidio of Monterey and Fort Hunter Liggett.

Meanwhile, Moore's son Steve decided to follow in his father's footsteps to West Point. Young Steve reported to Beast Barracks in the summer of 1971, one among nearly a thousand new cadets with the Class of 1975. But while his son adjusted to the rigors of Plebe year, Moore continued to tackle the problems of an Army plagued by "Vietnam Syndrome." As it were, Korea had been merely a snapshot of the greater issues facing the Army. In Europe, forty percent of American soldiers admitted to using drugs—mostly hashish and heroin. Barracks became war zones in their own right as soldiers formed their own gangs. Desertion and violent crime were on the rise. To make matters worse, officers, non-commissioned officers, and even their families were being attacked by renegade soldiers. By the latter the years of Vietnam, "fragging" (i.e. murdering unpopular leaders with fragmentation grenades) had become a regular occurrence. In fact, the Army documented nearly 800 fragging incidents between 1969 and 1971.

As Americans turned against the war, and took out their collective frustration on the military, morale and discipline within the Army plummeted. During Joe Galloway's third assignment to Vietnam, he recounted many of these frightening trends in a letter he wrote to Hal Moore:

March 26, 1971
Dear Hal:
A note to tell you that I had the opportunity to pay my first visit to Vietnam in almost five years, in late Feb and early this month.

Went over for about three weeks emergency duty during the Laotian operation. Spent about 10 days rotating around Quang Tri, Khe Sanh. One trip across the border.

Quite honestly, it is a totally different war and a totally different American Army, what I saw of it. I don't believe I would accept any sort of field command there, were I you. The name of the game is avoidance of combat. And considering the preparedness and morale of the troops it is just as well. Damned if I'd want to go for a walk in the sun with them.

At 1 a.m. a friend walked the two miles from the Quang Tri air terminal to the press billet, crossing two runways, paralleling the helicopter line, passing among about 50 choppers and by supply depots. He was not challenged a single time and saw no sentries.

Total lack of fire discipline, with doped up guards squirting off flares and shooting up the friendly bushes to see the pretty lights. Black GIs going thru long involved black power identification rituals. And when these troops refuse orders, which they are increasingly given to do, their commander is relieved.

Generational politics and conflicts aside, it seems to me it is incumbent on a soldier in a combat zone to be a very good soldier. The rest are just committing suicide.

Anyway, Hal, knowing your love of good soldiers and your enthusiasm for good soldiering, Vietnam these days should be avoided.

There is, in addition, today a great festering hostility between command and press which has replaced the camaraderie and mutual respect of other days. MACV was determined that the Laotian operation not be covered. Chopper rides forbidden to press. TOCs [tactical operations centers] ringed by guards with orders to turn away all civilians. US personnel under command-imposed rules not to talk to newsmen. Switch operators under instructions to handle press phone calls at a priority one below that of military routine. And on the other side of the coin are newsmen infuriated and eager to retaliate by seeing even the few rays of light in shades of black.

No war is good but all wars are fought either well or poorly. Once we fought this war well, now we fight it poorly. It may be a decade or two before Vietnam can be judged as a global strategic victory or defeat. There is misery and a seedling defeat in the fact that regardless of that judgment, we sent to this war an army which could fight well and brought home an army that fought poorly. The army's anguish is only the beginning. There've always been far too many parallels for comfort between the French experience and the American experience in Indochina. Let us hope that it does not extend to the postwar stresses on the military and the angry reaction.

Anyway, let me know how things are going with you and whether there is any chance of bumping into you in Singapore or Bangkok before too many months.

Best Regards,
Joe Galloway[212]

Taken together, these trends had produced an Army ill-prepared to fight and unprepared to win. As Moore took command of the Army Training Center, he knew it would take a lot of work to undo the costly damage of the Vietnam era.

In the early 1970s, the Army held Basic Training at six Army Training Centers throughout the US: Fort Dix, New Jersey; Fort Knox, Kentucky; Fort Polk, Louisiana; Fort McClellan, Alabama; Fort Leonard Wood, Missouri; and Fort Ord, California. In preparation for the end of the draft, Army leaders decided to launch a test program known as Project VOLAR (Volunteer Army). By changing several aspects of the Basic Training system, the Army hoped to attract more recruits and improve the retention rates among first-term enlistees. In addition to the Basic Training experiment, VOLAR included programs to improve professionalism, eliminate classroom instruction in favor of "hands-on" practical training, and provide better working conditions for soldiers.

While VOLAR went a long way towards improving the Army's readiness and overall professionalism, Hal noticed that several of its concepts were flawed. For instance, VOLAR had compromised many of the Army's long-standing traditions for building good discipline. Grooming standards had been relaxed, Reveille formations had been abolished, marching and close-order drill had been curtailed, beer was being served in the barracks, and a new "Enlisted Man's Council" allowed soldiers to circumvent the chain of command. VOLAR had even adopted the new recruiting slogan "The Army Wants to Join You," and barracks were being painted in pastel colors.

Hal realized that these new permissive attitudes had threatened the NCOs' role of enforcing discipline and "some [NCOs] became lax in the enforcement of existing rules and regulations." Because Basic Training was supposed to instill discipline and teamwork, Moore decided to change Fort Ord's role in the VOLAR program. "First," he explained, "great emphasis was placed on non-commissioned officer authority, responsibility, and performance." It was a nod to one the earliest leadership lessons he had learned in the Army— *push the power down*. He knew that since soldiers worked directly for non-commissioned officers, that the "responsibilities of Fort Ord's drill sergeants and other NCOs had to be increased." Second, he reinitiated the same officer

Hal Moore warms up for the opening pitch of the local Little League season. Moore strove to maintain good relations with the surrounding communities, which included San Francisco, Oakland, Salinas, Carmel, and Seaside, California. *The Hal Moore Collection*

Training on the M-60 Machine Gun. Heavy machine gun training was one of many subjects Moore added to the Basic Training curriculum at Fort Ord. He hoped to create a program that would give all soldiers a strong foundation in infantry weapons and tactics, particularly given the nature of combat in Vietnam. *US Army photo*

and NCO leadership courses he had used in Korea. Under his direction, the Fort Ord Leadership Academy became the nucleus for officer and NCO development. Its purpose, Hal said, was to "improve leadership skills and to develop technical and administrative abilities." Third, Hal placed a greater emphasis on physical training and mental discipline. "Rigorous physical demands were placed on all," he said, "and traditional Army discipline such as saluting and precision marching, close order drill, proper wearing of the uniform, and related military customs and courtesies were stressed."[213]

Almost simultaneously, Moore revised Fort Ord's Basic Training curriculum. In the early days of VOLAR, bayonet training, hand-to-hand combat, obstacle courses, and speed road marches had been abolished. Moore, however, reinstituted each of these subjects during his first year of command. "The goal was for every man leaving Basic Combat Training to be in the best physical shape of his life and to know it . . . to stretch his mind and his muscles and to assist him in thereby gaining more pride in himself, more self-confidence, and above all, more self-discipline." Moore's philosophy was simple: a man who had more self-discipline had more confidence in his ability to do the job. Likewise, "men in a unit which has disciplined, competent leaders will have more confidence in those leaders."[214]

Moore also revised the weapons training for his recruits. Up to that point, Basic Training had covered only two weapons: the M16 rifle and the M26 hand grenade—there had been no instruction in heavy infantry weapons, survival tactics, or land mine warfare. Instead, the Army had transferred these topics to Advanced Individual Training (AIT) for Combat Arms soldiers (e.g. infantry, mechanized cavalry scouts, tank crewmen, etc). Moore's approach, however, added training on the M203 Grenade Launcher, M60 Machine Gun, M72A2 Light Anti-Tank Weapon (bazooka), the Claymore Mine, and introduced survival and evasion tactics to the curriculum. "The transfer of these subjects," he said, "produced both immediate and 'down-stream' advantages." After all, in a war like Vietnam, where there were no frontlines and no rear echelons, non-combat soldiers could benefit from learning more than just the standard M-16 rifle.[215]

In the fall of 1971, Moore's training revisions were given a forum at the Modern Volunteer Army Conference at Fort Jackson, South Carolina. Commanders and representatives from each of the Army's training centers convened to give their assessment of the VOLAR program and provide any recommendations for improvement. "Fort Ord's views," he recalled, "were favorably received and the revised Army training programs published in 1972 made provisions for increased training." This not to say that Moore was solely responsible for the Army's Basic Training overhaul—there were several recommendations made by the various VOLAR players. There can be little argument, however, that Moore's experiments and recommendations had a profound impact on the Basic Training and AIT programs. In fact, "shifting heavy weapons familiarization and survival tactics to Basic Training allowed the Advanced Individual Training course to use the freed time to expand instruction in the remaining subjects, add new subjects, and still stay within the allotted training period."[216]

A trainee prepares to throw his first live hand grenade during Basic Training at Ford Ord, 1972. *US Army photo*

Moore hosts General (ret) Omar Bradley, the former Army Chief of Staff and famed World War II commander, for a gala event at Fort Ord, 1972. Omar Bradley had handed Moore his diploma when the latter walked across the stage on his Graduation Day from West Point in 1945. *The Hal Moore Collection*

Hal and Julie attend a military ball for the 49th Infantry Brigade. February 19, 1972. *The Hal Moore Collection*

Moore inspects the troops during one of his final Pass and Review ceremonies at Fort Ord, 1973. *The Hal Moore Collection*

Moore is inducted as an "Honorary NCO" by the members of the Fort Ord chapter of the Noncommissioned Officers' Association, 1972. Moore's NCOs were so impressed by his dedication to the troops and his love of training, that they nominated him for the honorary membership. *The Hal Moore Collection*

Basic trainees prepare for their graduation parade, 1972. During Moore's command tenure, he reversed many of VOLAR's early programs which undermined the Army's traditions for building good discipline. *US Army photo*

Moore receives his third star on December 5, 1974. Following his promotion to Lieutenant General, Moore became the Army Deputy Chief of Staff for Personnel. *The Hal Moore Collection*

Despite these remarkable developments, Moore still lived in an era of anti-war protests, "and California," he said, "was a hotbed of anti-war activity." Shortly after he took command of the Army Training Center, actress Jane Fonda (whose fraternizing tour of North Vietnam had earned her the nickname "Hanoi Jane") arrived at the gates of Fort Ord with her anti-war group, "Free the Army," or FTA, in tow. "Of course there would be TV cameras present and I knew they wanted a photogenic confrontation between soldiers with fixed bayonets . . . and the flower-power children. I gave instructions that the MPs and civilian gate guards were to stand in front of the gate but there was to be no use of force and no weapons or nightsticks in hand. Not even the most rabid of demonstrators found much joy in the non-confrontation. The TV cameras left and soon the crowd broke up, furious at our pacifism. Later that day, Ms. Fonda somehow gained entrance and was found in the recreation room of one of my training center barracks talking with new soldiers. My MPs quietly and courteously escorted her off the post.[217]

"On another occasion, I got wind of a large group of protestors who were headed to the other gate of Fort Ord, which was at the city of Seaside, California." Hoping to diffuse the situation before it even started, Hal directed the Provost Marshal to post the oldest, most out-of-shape, civilian gate guard at the entrance. He was ordered just to "stand there silently with his hands folded across his back. No weapon or nightstick on his belt." Arriving at the gate, the protestors were dumbfounded to see a dainty little man who was old enough to be their grandfather. Realizing that they couldn't bring themselves to attack the old man, the crowd quickly dispersed. Little did they know, however, that just around the corner, a platoon of MPs lay waiting with fully loaded M-16s, ready to disperse the crowd if things got too out of hand. "In those years, we dealt with many anti-war protests. It was an interesting time to command an Army post." Yet whenever a group of demonstrators showed up, Moore's guidance was always the same: "Don't overreact." He knew it would only play into the hands of the larger anti-war movement.[218]

Diffusing anti-war demonstrations, however, was only part of Hal Moore's larger community relations program. In the spirit of building better ties with the local community, Hal put together several "activity days" where people from across the state could come and observe Basic Training. He had noticed that there was a great lack of understanding about the VOLAR programs among local civilians and retired veterans. "It was apparent that the more sensational (and least successful) test programs had received most of the publicity while the real accomplishments and efforts to improve professionalism and Army life had been largely ignored." Moore invited several community leaders and journalists from nearby cities including San Francisco, Oakland, Seaside, and Monterey to "see where the troops lived, eat with the troops, even talk with the soldiers privately. I welcomed the reporters in particular and saw to it that they could go anywhere they wanted and talk with anyone on post." His only guidance was that they not interfere with training.[219]

Moore also made great strides to improve the quality of life for everyone on post. In 1971, he oversaw the grand opening of the Fort Ord Welcome Center, which housed "all possible facilities and services relating to the arrival or departure of people at [Ford Ord]." This Welcome Center provided services for finance, housing, personnel, and even a registration office for youth activities—which included "a variety of year-round sports and recreational programs." Volunteer Army wives staffed the Army Community Service office at the Welcome Center to assist incoming families. "One of their helpful services," Moore said, "was lending such useful items as pots and pans and playpens to new families."[220]

There was, however, a lingering issue of crime on post. "No other improvements in Army life can be truly effective," said Moore, "if a safe, disciplined environment is not provided for soldiers and their families." The Vietnam War era had seen a dramatic increase in on-post crime rates, and Fort Ord had been no exception. To combat the problem, Moore increased the number of MP patrols, adopted a strict "zero tolerance" policy on drugs, and established various neighborhood councils to keep an eye out for criminal activity. Under these security measures, the crime rate at Fort Ord dropped considerably.[221]

In August 1973, Hal returned to Washington, DC: first as the Commanding General of the Army Personnel Center (1973–74), then as the Deputy Chief of Staff for Personnel (1974–77). In both capacities, he remained at the forefront of the Army's struggle to maintain its end-strength and attract quality recruits. As Deputy Chief of Staff, Moore petitioned Congress to extend enlistment bonuses for combat arms soldiers. Since the end of Vietnam, the Army had been under pressure from Congress and the Department of Defense to curtail its enlistment bonus program.[222]

Testifying before the House Appropriations Committee in May 1975, Moore told Congressional leaders that although the Army had met its recruiting goals for the fiscal year, it would be much harder to meet the same quota without extending bonuses for those joining the combat arms (infantry, armor, and artillery). Traditionally, these MOSs were the hardest ones to fill with voluntary enlistments. Now that the draft was gone, the Army had to create incentives to keep a steady stream of recruits in their core combat specialties. "No shortfall is anticipated in FY [Fiscal Year] 76 and beyond," Moore told Congress, "providing we continue to receive your support for the combat arms enlistment bonus." After all, the deck was normally stacked against the combat arms community, "because young men are more interested in learning skills that they can use to earn a living after they leave the Army."[223]

When he wasn't fighting to keep enlistment bonuses, however, Moore was operating at the other end of the personnel spectrum: overseeing the Reduction-in-Force (RIF) boards. Following the end of the draft, Congress reduced the Army's end-strength to 785,000 from 1,163,338. Attempting to normalize the postwar rank structure, these RIF boards selected several officers and warrant officers for early separation. "Some other major actions were opening up duty positions to women which would make them vulnerable to

General and Mrs. Moore in the receiving line at President Carter's Inaugural Ball, January 22, 1977. *The Hal Moore Collection*

become wartime casualties and correcting Retired Pay Inversion."[224]

However, as Moore settled in to his final tour at the Pentagon, the Republic of Vietnam finally imploded. Per the Paris Peace Accords, US forces withdrew from South Vietnam in 1973. North and South had also agreed to retain their respective border along the 17th Parallel. However, the North Vietnamese never intended to stand by their end of the bargain. Once Hanoi realized that the US would not intervene militarily, the NVA launched a full-scale invasion of South Vietnam in early 1975. In response, ARVN troops mounted an unsuccessful defense before re-

Moore's command portrait at the Army Personnel Center in Alexandria, Virgina, 1974. *The Hal Moore Collection*

treating through Hue, Da Nang, and finally, Da Lat. With the North Vietnamese closing in on Saigon, the ARVN made its final stand at the Battle of Xuan Loc. As NVA tanks rolled into Saigon on the morning of April 30, 1975, the South Vietnamese government finally surrendered.

Watching these events unfold from his post in Washington, Hal Moore was incredulous. In Vietnam, the US had won every battle, yet somehow managed to lose the war. After nearly a decade of misguided war policies— and over 58,000 combat deaths—America had abandoned an ally which she had promised to defend. Watching the last helicopter evacuate from the rooftop of the American Embassy in Saigon, it seemed as though the entire war—the bloodshed, the sacrifice, and the untold cost in human suffering— had been an exercise in futility.

In the spring of 1977, Army Chief of Staff, General Bernard Rogers, tapped Moore to become the Commanding General of US Army, Japan. However, "for personal reasons, I elected to retire instead." Hal Moore retired on August 1, 1977—completing thirty-two years of active service.[225]

Keeping a time-honored tradition. Moore raises the American flag over the new deck at his home in Crested Butte. It was often said that the residents of Crested Butte knew when Moore was in town by whether or not his flag was flying. *The Bill Moore Collection*

CHAPTER EIGHT

WHEN WAR IS DONE

U pon his retirement, Moore began a second career as the Vice President of the Crested Butte Ski Resort in Crested Butte, Colorado. For the next several years, he and Julie maintained two homes: one in Colorado; the other in Auburn, Alabama—a picturesque college town forty miles west of Fort Benning, Georgia. As Moore settled into his retired life, however, he and Joe Galloway took on a monumental new project.

After Ia Drang, Hal and Joe discussed the possibility of writing a book about their battlefield experiences. "But," as Hal admitted, "we each had our careers, and as I moved up the ranks and Joe remained overseas doing three more tours in Vietnam . . . that plan remained on the backburner for both of us." The first opportunity either of them had to discuss the project at length was in November 1976. Joe had arrived in Washington, DC en route to his

Moore's retirement home in Crested Butte, Colorado. Following his retirement from the Army, Moore became the Vice President of the Crested Butte Ski Resort. *The Bill Moore Collection*

new assignment as the UPI bureau chief in Moscow. When the two met for dinner at Moore's home in nearby Fort Myer, they agreed that they would begin working on the book after Moore retired and Galloway returned from overseas.[226]

"Early one morning in January 1982," Hal said, "after Joe had come home ... [he] called and asked if I was ready to begin serious work on the book." It turned out that Joe had recently seen the film *More American Graffiti*. During the film, one of its central characters was shown fighting as a soldier in Vietnam. Rekindling those horrific memories of the Ia Drang Valley, Joe openly wept and felt that the only to deal with his angst was to write their story of the battle. On that January morning, Hal and Joe began making phone calls and wrote a questionnaire to send to the surviving Ia Drang veterans. Little did they realize that their endeavor would take them nearly a decade to complete.[227]

While gathering data for his book, however, Moore had the opportunity to do something unprecedented in American military history. In September 1989, the sixty-seven-year-old Moore participated in a joint Soviet-American hike through the Tien Shan Mountains of Kazakhstan and Uzbekistan. The hike itself was a goodwill event catering specifically to American veterans of the Vietnam War and Soviet veterans of their recent war in Afghanistan. Ten years earlier, the Soviets had invaded Afghanistan to facilitate the socialist government's counterinsurgency against the Mujahideen. In doing so, the Russians found themselves embroiled in a bloody, nine-year conflict which depleted much of their military resources. By 1988, under a collapsing economy and unable to crush the Afghan resistance, the Soviets conceded the fight and withdrew from Afghanistan.

Meanwhile, the frost of the Cold War had begun to thaw as the US and USSR moved toward a friendlier and more cooperative relationship. During this time of dialogue, the two superpowers learned that they had much in common with their respective wars in Vietnam and Afghanistan. Both wars had been unpopular at home and both had been prosecuted with unclear objectives. Both countries had, to varying degrees, supported the enemies of the other. Moreover, the veterans of both conflicts had returned home to a society which either ignored them or castigated them. Looking forward to a new era of friendship, East and West came together for one of the first goodwill events of the post-Cold War era.

Moore's involvement began on April 30, 1989. Early that morning, he received a call from Bob Rheault, one of his West Point classmates. Over the phone, Rheault explained the nature of the event and asked Moore if he would like to attend. Without hesitation, Hal said he was definitely interested and that he would get back to Rheault soon. "I hung up and slowly turned to my wife Julie. She, early on, had sensed that something very surprising, very unusual was in the wind, and had picked up on my end of the conversation. Before I could say a word, she said, 'I don't know what that was all about, but from listening and looking at your eyes, go for it!'"[228]

Within five minutes, Moore was back on the phone with Rheault and confirmed his spot on the American delegation. "Four months after that phone call, muddle-headed from four days of jetlag under my belt, badly in need of sleep and exercise, I was airborne over Russia on a dismal Aeroflot Redeye looking out a window at the sun rising over the steppes of Central Asia." It was now mid-morning on September 6, 1989 and Moore was touching down in the fabled city of Tashkent, Uzbek SSR. Together with thirteen other Vietnam veterans and two interpreters, Hal Moore greeted his Soviet comrades on the sunny tarmac.[229]

"I recall that initial, strained meeting between us and the Soviets—the TV cameras, the interviews." Indeed, the local state-run media had flooded the airport to cover the arrival of these American veterans. "I had studied the Russian language for four months," Moore recalled, "but very little of it came to the front of my head at the time. How tired I was."[230]

Leaving the airport, the American-Soviet gang stopped by a local restaurant where they enjoyed a hearty breakfast that was plentiful even by American standards—"three eggs, sunny side up . . . with cold cuts, cheeses, delicious round bread, real butter, and tea. The thought crossed my mind that these folks don't pay much attention to cholesterol. If there were any lingering doubts that I was in the Orient, they were quickly dispelled when I went into the men's room and spotted the toilets. They were two feet by one foot, cylindrically-shaped holes in the floor over a pit—exactly like the toilets in Japan where I served on occupation duty from '45–'48."[231]

On their way to the expedition's base camp in Chimgan, they passed by an impressive, multi-storied stone building—perhaps the nicest structure Moore had yet seen in Tashkent. Asking the group what the building was, one Russian replied "KGB Offices." The building itself was a touch of irony: in a city dominated by cheap government building projects, the Communists had reserved the best construction for their own party apparatchiks. Just one more incongruity within the Soviet system.

That night at the base camp, around the campfire, the American and Soviet veterans enjoyed another hearty meal and sang songs of their respective homelands. Moore remarked that nearly every other Russian in the group knew how to play the guitar. "Their warm, sincere, hospitality and friendliness was upfront and solid." For years, he had been trained to see the Soviets as enemies; now, he was glad to meet them as friends. The following day, they began the first leg of their journey into the mountains. "That started the sealing of the team," Moore said. "Everyone got along great." Moore marveled at how physically fit the Soviets were. "I was surprised to see, however, that most were cigarette smokers; no lung cancer worries there!"[232]

Moore (back row, standing left) relaxes with a few of his American and Soviet comrades, near Chimgan, Uzbek SSR. *The Hal Moore Collection*

The first leg of the hike took them through the grassy valley of the Tien Shan wilderness, up the foothills and around the highland lakes. On their first night out, the group stopped at what Hal called the "Frozen Brook Bivuoac." They had ventured into the piney forests of the upper Tien Shan and their new campsite lay on the banks of a bustling creek. "The unspoiled beauty of that lovely birch grove with its inter-winding small creeks" made for a beautiful campsite, but because the group had hiked to a considerably higher altitude, the night wind dropped the temperature to 26°F, freezing the brook to a standstill.[233]

The next day, Moore reached the top of Nahota Pass, elevation 12,600 feet, overlooking the route into Kazakhstan. "My sweetest memory, so good

Moore poses with his fellow American and Soviet veterans during their goodwill hike through the Tien Shan Mountains in Uzbekistan and Kazakhstan, September 1989. *The Hal Moore Collection*

One of the several "rocky lakes" which Moore described seeing on his trek through the Uzbek wilderness. *The Hal Moore Collection*

The view outside Moore's hotel window of Tashkent, Uzbek SSR. In a city dominated by cheap government projects, Moore noticed that the finest construction and craftsmanship had been reserved for the KGB offices. *The Hal Moore Collection*

The sixty-seven-year-old Hal Moore conquers the Nahota Pass at an elevation of 12,600 feet. One of the younger Soviet veterans was so impressed by Moore's strength and endurance that he volunteered to serve under Moore if he ever took another command. *The Hal Moore Collection*

to dwell on, is of the emotional celebration at the top of the pass, and the sense of history being made. The feeling of brotherhood. The cook pots were soon boiling and we toasted our team's accomplishment with hot green tea . . . which refreshed and renewed us all throughout the entire trek. Then, after some hot jamming by guitar, harmonica, and clapping, there was a reading in English and Russian of the written fact of our accomplishment, which was then placed in a waterproof container under a rock cairn." The message read:

> In the spirit of Soviet-American friendship and international under-standing, the veterans of Afghanistan and Vietnam record their con-quest of this mountain that the desire for conquest in war may perish from this land that we have learned to love and from all lands forever. Sept. 11, 1989.[234]

Down the mountain pass and into Kazakhstan, the group settled into another bivouac along a tree-lined lake. "Then, there was the special evening meal taken together in a circle and the group singing. I was surprised by the Soviets' continued requests for us to sing 'America the Beautiful' and 'This Land is Your Land' and 'God Bless America'—which we did. I requested again that the Soviets sing their own song 'Meadowland'—beautiful, stirring, and which I recall hearing on the radio many times on 'VE Day' in May 1945. That night, that bugle playing 'Taps' was a bittersweet time for us all. We all

Moore with comrades Sergei (left) and Costei (right) at the top of Nahota Pass into Kazakh SSR. Hal recalled that both the young Soviets were paratroopers and Costei was an accomplished skier. *The Hal Moore Collection*

knew that the beating heart of the great adventure was slowly pulsing down to its end." During their final night out, Moore approached a Soviet paratrooper, soliciting a pair of Soviet jump wings. Moore's youngest son David, then 28, was serving in the 82nd Airborne Division and had given his father a pair of US jump wings in the hopes of eliciting such a trade. The Russian paratrooper, a young Muscovite named Sasha, happily traded his wings. When Moore mentioned that his son was in the 82nd Airborne, Sasha confessed that his unit had often conducted wargames against other Soviet formations playing the role of the 82nd Airborne.[235]

As the group returned to the city, they split up into hotel rooms and "visiting the sights, we knew it wouldn't be the same. It would soon be over. Vietnam Vets and Soviet Vets had joined together in a successful, innovative, physically-demanding team undertaking for the common greater cause of better understanding and peace between America and the Soviet Union."[236]

Moore was one of five American veterans selected by the Soviet government to fly back to Moscow on the first Redeye out of Tashkent that Friday night, September 15. He got to the airport early, where nearly all of the Afghan vets had gathered to see him off. Most of them were wearing their commemorative Vietnam/Afghan T-shirt. They were so impressed by Moore's strength and endurance that one of them volunteered to serve under Moore if he ever took another command. "When called into the baggage check-in, our Soviet comrades were so concerned that we be handled properly that they bulled in,

Visiting an Afghan War memorial. As the frost of the Cold War thawed, the US and USSR discovered that they had much in common with their respective "proxy wars." *The Hal Moore Collection*

dominated the women behind the counter and literally took over." Moore stood there in shock as the Soviet veterans proceeded to tag his luggage and thrust it onto the conveyor belt. "Can anyone imagine that happening in a US Airport?" Moore asked.

The Americans and Soviets shared an emotional round of hugs and final goodbyes. Hal remembered that "honest tears were shed" as the two groups parted and other passengers looked on with curiosity. "We were then told it was time to leave, to get on the bus for the plane. As we walked out into the warm, deepening twilight through the trees towards the bus, we looked back to the fence where our comrades were now standing and waving." Moore and his friends waved back shouting "dosvidanya!" and "spasiba!" ("goodbye" and "thank you"). The Soviets shouted in reply, "Remember! Remember! Remember!" It was one of the most touching moments in Moore's life.[237]

Meanwhile, Hal's youngest son, David, carried on the family's tradition of military service. Like his father and elder brother, David attended West Point—graduating with the Class of 1984. As a young Captain, Dave Moore jumped into Panama with the 82nd Airborne Division for Operation Just Cause and was among the first troops to arrive in Saudi Arabia during the buildup to the Gulf War. In January 1991, Joe Galloway—still covering the world's conflicts—was on his way to the Persian Gulf. He phoned Hal and Julie to tell them that he would be out of contact for the duration of the war. During their conversation, however, Joe was surprised to hear Julie say how

Moore and a fellow Vietnam vet take a tour of Moscow before returning to the United States, September 1989. *The Hal Moore Collection*

worried she was that "Davey" was on the frontlines of this new war. Surely, Joe said, after years of seeing her father and husband go off to war, she would be used to these emotions by now. Julie's answer was stern, yet succinct:

> Joe Galloway, you don't understand one damn thing about this. You can replace a husband, but you can never replace a son![238]

Fortunately, Dave made it through Desert Storm without a scratch and remained on active duty, for twenty-seven years—retiring in 2011 at the rank of Colonel.

Ironically, it was during the Gulf War that Hal and Joe made their biggest stride toward completing their book. In August 1990, Joe (now working for *US News and World Report*) pitched an idea to his editor for a cover article commemorating the twenty-fifth anniversary of Ia Drang. Joe's timing was impeccable as the US military was in opening stages of Desert Shield and the country's mood was decidedly different than it had been during Vietnam. In fact, it seemed as though Americans collectively felt guilty for how they had treated their Vietnam veterans, and were determined to make up for it. American flags unfurled in lawns across the country and care packages addressed to "Any Soldier" flowed into Saudi Arabia by the thousands. Joe's article, which appeared in the October 29, 1990 issue of *US News and World Report*, was such a success that it earned him a National Magazine Award. At the award ceremony in 1991, Joe was cornered by Harry Evans, a former *US News* editor and then-president of Random House. Evans wasted no time.

"I want that book," he told Galloway.

"What book?"

"The book you are going to write on the Ia Drang battles. I don't even need an outline. Your article is outline enough."[239]

Evans editorial insight paid off. On November 11, 1992, *We Were Soldiers Once . . . and Young* debuted to critical acclaim and quickly rose to the top of the *New York Times* bestseller list. But for Hal Moore, the process of bringing closure to his ordeal in the Ia Drang Valley was far from over. Throughout the 1990s, Moore and Galloway would return to Vietnam several times—both of them eager to walk the battlefields they had once known.

Their first trips back to Vietnam—in 1990 and 1991 to research the book—were confounded by Hanoi's bureaucracy. As a journalist, Joe was able to get a visa without issue, but Hanoi was deeply suspicious of Moore. Why would an American general want to visit Vietnam fifteen years after the fall of Saigon? they wondered. Hal finally obtained a visa after some backdoor politicking in Thailand (as Australian businessman in Bangkok had political connections to Hanoi) but his request to return to the Ia Drang Valley was roundly ignored.

These visits did, however, gain Moore an audience with General Vo

Hanoi street scene during Moore and Galloway's first return trip to Vietnam, September 1990. *The Hal Moore Collection*

Nguyen Giap, formerly the supreme commander of the North Vietnamese Army, and Major General Hoang Phoung, "the official historian of the Vietnamese Army, who as a lieutenant colonel was sent down the Ho Chi Minh Trail to write a lessons-learned report on the Pleiku Campaign." Phuong told Moore that the NVA had been studying American tactics ever since the Marines waded ashore at Da Nang. However, the arrival of US airmobile forces changed the equation. Phuong said that the helicopters had made life very difficult for the NVA and Viet Cong. "You jumped all over," Phuong said, "like a frog, even into the rear area of our troops . . . you created disorder among our troops." According to Phuong, the heliborne operations had forced the NVA to retreat from the Plei Me area in smaller groups. Moore also had the chance to meet his opposing commanders from the Ia Drang battle. "Their comments and answers to our questions," he said "were a vital part of our research."[240]

Moore's persistence in returning to Ia Drang finally paid off in 1993. In the intervening time since his and Galloway's last visits, a number of world events had changed Hanoi's attitude. The Soviet Union had collapsed in December 1991 and China was making long strides toward a capitalist economy. Also, the rise of capitalist neighbors such as Thailand, Singapore, and Malaysia had put the pressure on Vietnam to modernize its economy and throw its hat into the free trade market. Then too, Hanoi also wanted to normalize relations with the US and "were seeking foreign investment and most-

Moore and Galloway stroll through the Vietnamese Air Force Museum in Hanoi, November 1991. *The Hal Moore Collection*

favored-nation trade terms." However, it was the release of *We Were Soldiers Once . . . and Young* that finally put Hanoi's suspicions to rest. They now realized that Moore and Galloway had no ulterior motives.[241]

Another factor which helped Moore in his quest to return to Ia Drang was a solicitation from ABC Television. Shortly after the release of *We Were Soldiers Once . . . and Young,* the producer of ABC's *Day One* program (now defunct) approached Moore and Galloway with an offer to make a documentary of the battle. The film would include studio interviews and a trip back to the battlefield. Accompanying Hal and Joe on this studio-funded trip would be Command Sergeant Major (ret) Basil Plumley; Tony Nadal and John Herren, both of whom had been company commanders at LZ X-Ray; Bruce Crandall, the helicopter ace; Bill Beck, the courageous machine gunner who held off an entire battalion with his M60; Ernie Savage, who as a buck sergeant rallied the "Lost Platoon" after his lieutenant and senior NCOs were killed; *Day One*'s anchorman Forrest Sawyer; the producer Terry Wrong; and associated production crew.

The day after their arrival in Vietnam, Hal, Joe, and their entourage met with General Nguyen Huu An, his former subordinate officers, and a group of Vietnamese veterans for dinner at a large floating restaurant on Hanoi's West Lake. Hal recalled that many of these old veterans were crippled, "missing arms, legs, eyes. Their wheelchairs were crude and decrepit, as were the prosthetics replacing their missing arms and legs." However, upon seeing their

Moore sits with Major General Hoang Phuong and Joe Galloway in Hanoi, 1990. *The Hal Moore Collection*

American counterparts, the Vietnamese warmly smiled and held up a sign which read, in English, "Welcome American Veterans." Throughout the evening, there was no talk of who had won or who had lost the war. All were happy just to dine as friends.[242]

Early the next morning, at 4:15 a.m., Moore, Galloway, the other American veterans, and the *Day One* crew, hopped a flight to Da Nang "where our journey to the Central Highlands would begin." Accompanied by General An, Moore and his comrades climbed aboard four chartered buses and began their journey heading south along Highway 1. For Hal Moore, the road trip was much like stepping into a time machine. Highway 1 had been the site of several Viet Cong ambushes during the war. Now, nearly two decades after the fall of Saigon, the road was safe to travel but had retained many of its wartime potholes and craters.[243]

On the first leg of their trip, they passed the site where the Chu Lai airbase had once been. "To see that big airbase the Marines had built here at Chu Lai had disappeared was stunning to Joe," Moore said. Joe had been with the Marines when they landed there in 1965 and had seen them clear a sizeable area to make room for the airbase. "Now it was gone as if it had never existed." But the Marine airbase wasn't the only American relic which had been dismantled following the US departure. In fact, it seemed as though every bit of American infrastructure had been taken down. The bases, buildings, and barracks which had housed some 3,000,000 US servicemen during the war had

Moore with General Chu Muy Man, the senior battlefield commander during the Ia Drang Campaign. *The Hal Moore Collection*

Moore, Galloway, the *Day One* crew, and the rest of the traveling party gather for a photo at LZ X-Ray, October 1993. *The Hal Moore Collection*

vanished without a trace. Oddly enough, the only fortifications that remained were those from the French occupation—every so often, Moore could see the concrete façade of a little Beau Geste fort. "I suppose the old forts were built too well to easily tear down, and there's no market for concrete rubble," he said. "Even the huge piles of war junk we left behind—blown up trucks and tanks, crashed aircraft, twisted steel runway plates—long ago disappeared into the holds of ships that carried it all away to Japanese steel smelters." Other pieces of American equipment—including bulldozers, cranes, backhoes, graders, and utility trucks—had been sold to pay off Hanoi's war debt. Toward the end of the day, the group passed through Bong Son, where Moore's brigade had conducted Operation Masher in 1966. And by nightfall, they had arrived in Qui Nhon, which had been the port-of-entry for all 1st Cavalry Division troopers in 1965.[244]

Their next stop the following morning was An Khe, "where we hoped to walk the division base camp we had hacked out of the jungle and scrub brush," but like the other American bases throughout Vietnam, An Khe too had been dismantled. The area now belonged to the headquarters of a Vietnamese reserve army division. When Moore and the group finally reached Pleiku, their chartered helicopter flight to Ia Drang was delayed by the Pleiku Province People's Committee. Apparently, Hanoi's clearance and General An's rank carried no weight among the Pleiku commissars. The local bureaucrats made it clear that *they* reserved the right to grant passage into the Ia Drang,

LZ X-Ray looking northwest from the former Charlie Company foxholes. The travel group's helicopter is visible in the background. *The Hal Moore Collection*

regardless of anything Hanoi said. "Over endless cups of green tea," Hal remembered, "we once again put our case for a historical return to the Ia Drang in company with General An." Satisfied with their story, the People's Committee Chief granted their request and cleared them to fly on October 18, 1993.[245]

On the morning of the 18th, an old Soviet Mi-24 helicopter arrived at the Pleiku airport to take Moore and his entourage back to the battlefields of Ia Drang. On the tarmac, the two Vietnamese pilots admitted that they had no idea where the Ia Drang Valley was. Moore pointed to a spot on the map, but it still wasn't enough for the pilots to get their bearings. Finally, Joe Galloway fished out his old Boy Scout compass and, with a general heading, they were on their way.

Once in the air, Moore looked out his window to find the Vietnamese countryside much the same as it had been twenty-eight years ago. After a few minutes, Moore drew a deep breath as he saw the old LZ X-Ray clearing at the foot of the Chu Pong Massif. As the helicopter settled over the clearing, Moore could see "clear signs that nature had done much to repair the devastation of war. Shattered trees had grown new branches. Shell holes and the line of old foxholes were at least partially filled. Elephant grass had reclaimed large swaths of land that had been burned over by fires set by napalm and bombs and artillery shells."[246]

Setting foot once again onto the old battleground, Moore felt a tingling sense of peace. In his mind's eye, he could see his young troopers fanning out

Old enemies become friends at LZ X-Ray. Moore shakes hands with General An during their return visit to X-Ray, October 1993. *The Hal Moore Collection*

into their tactical formations—awaiting contact with an enemy that lurked somewhere beyond the tree line. For years, he had felt the urge to return to these battlefields. Now, twenty-eight years later, he finally felt the soothing sensation of bringing closure to the most chaotic chapter of his life. He could never forget the horrors of that three-day battle; nor could he forget the sting of carrying a lifeless trooper in his arms. Yet somehow, returning to this battleground brought him a sense of peace he had not felt in years.

Every man in the party ventured to where he had been during the fateful battle. Moore returned to the termite mound which had been his command post. Although heavy foliage had taken over most of the mound, Moore recognized his old CP in an instant. Tony Nadal and John Herren wandered over to the creek bed where their companies had held off a ferocious enemy determined to outflank them. Meanwhile, Bill Beck made his way to the spot where, with his lone machine gun, he had destroyed an entire enemy battalion. Moore recalled that Beck, as an assistant machine gunner, "had inherited the machine gun that first day of the battle when his gunner and best friend from back home in Pennsylvania, Russell Adams, was shot in the head." Miraculously, Adams survived the gunshot wound, but Beck was haunted by the memory of picking up Russell's helmet and finding a portion of his brain in it.[247]

As Beck surveyed the site, he noticed a small metal object lodged in the ground. Curious to see what it was, he nudged it with his boot and discovered that it was "the remains of an American steel helmet." Convinced that it was part of Adams' old helmet, Beck scooped it up and quietly slipped it into his backpack. Not far behind, Ernie Savage—with Nadal and Herren in tow—went to the small knoll where he had held together the "Lost Platoon" after Lieutenant Herrick's last stand.[248]

Throughout the visit to Ia Drang, it was clear that the Vietnamese wanted to protect their guests. The Ia Drang Valley was only a stone's throw from the Cambodian border and the Khmer Rouge guerrillas had been launching raids into southern Vietnam for years. Intelligence from Hanoi suggested that a faction of the Khmer Rouge had taken shelter in the Chu Pong Massif, just up the slope from LZ X-Ray. Thus, Moore, Galloway, General An, the other Ia Drang vets, and the *Day One* crew had to spend the day under the watchful eye of a Vietnamese Army platoon called in from its border guard duty.

As the day drew to a close, Hal gathered the veterans—American and Vietnamese—into a circle and, with heads bowed, he offered the following prayer:

> Let us stand in silence, in prayer, in memory of the men on both sides, Vietnamese and American, who died on this ground, in this place, in November of 1965. May they rest in peace.[249]

When the circle broke, General An approached Moore and, in a brotherly embrace, An kissed Moore on both cheeks. "Old enemies can become friends," Moore later said.

Hal Moore in front of the termite mound which doubled as his command post during the Battle of Ia Drang. By the time he returned to X-Ray in the 1990s, the mound had been taken over by heavy foliage. *The Hal Moore Collection*

That night, Moore, Galloway, and the American veterans spent the night at LZ X-Ray. By the dim light of a campfire, Moore walked the battlefield while his comrades slept peacefully. Throughout the night, he wandered through the places where his men had made history on those fateful November days: the creek bed, the termite mound, the Charlie Company foxholes, and the site of Jack Geoghegan's last stand. With every step, he could feel the souls that still lingered on the battlefield—the souls of his beloved troopers—the souls of men who were among the first of 58,256 lives lost to that terrible conflict. On that night, twenty-eight years after the opening volleys of the Pleiku Campaign, Moore found the elusive peace he had been looking for.

The following morning, "as we gathered our packs and put out the fire," he said, "I thought about the magical night we had spent here and what it meant. I was convinced that all who had died in this place the Vietnamese called the Forest of Screaming Souls could at last be blessed with silence and we could go home with our measure of peace as well." Moore would return to Vietnam several times over the ensuing decade, including a visit to Dien Bien Phu with his wife Julie in 1999.[250]

In the intervening time, Hollywood screenwriter and producer Randall Wallace (whose works included *Braveheart* and *The Man in the Iron Mask*) picked up a copy of *We Were Soldiers Once . . . and Young*. Wallace had been touched by Moore's remark that Hollywood "had gotten it wrong every damned time"

The Moore boys in retirement (left to right): Ballard, Bill, and Hal, 1999. *The Ballard Moore Collection*

Hal Moore stands with Mel Gibson at the Hollywood premiere of *We Were Soldiers* on February 25, 2002. The film was released nation-wide released on March 1, 2002 and featured Gibson in the role of Hal Moore. *We Were Soldiers* grossed over $100,000,000 worldwide. *Photo by Greg DeGuire/Getty Images*

when making films about the Vietnam War. After reading Moore's book, Wallace was determined to make a movie that didn't portray the Vietnam veteran according to popular stereotypes.

With the backing of Paramount Pictures, Wallace wrote, produced, and even directed the film. Recalling their success with *Braveheart*, Wallace and the studio selected actor Mel Gibson for the role of Hal Moore. Following Gibson onto the set was an all-star supporting cast which included Madeline Stowe portraying Julie Moore and Sam Elliot in the role of Basil Plumley. Throughout pre-production, Wallace and the cast often met with Hal and Julie to discuss the script. During these visits, Hal remembered that Julie wasn't the least bit shy in giving advice to Randall Wallace on how to depict life on the home front. Wallace even let Hal serve as technical advisor while filming the battle scenes on location at Fort Hunter Liggett, California.

We Were Soldiers opened on March 1, 2002 to critical acclaim and grossed over $100,000,000 worldwide. Overall, Moore was satisfied with the film, saying that it was "about seventy-five percent accurate; twenty-five percent Hollywood." But admittedly, he didn't like much of the artistic license that Randall Wallace had taken. For instance, Rick Rescorla—the heroic platoon leader whose photo had appeared on the cover of *We Were Soldiers Once . . . and Young*—was completely written out of the film. The bayonet charge at the end of the film—depicting Moore leading his troops up a hill to destroy the Vietnamese reserve—never happened. One particular inaccuracy struck a tender nerve with Julie: she had wanted the film to show her and the other Army wives living in the low-rent neighborhoods and trailer parks in Columbus, "not living the life of Riley in spacious two-story homes on Colonel's Row at Fort Benning." Still, Hal Moore was pleased with the final product. "Hollywood finally got it right," he said. "They finally got it right."[251]

Following the premiere of *We Were Soldiers*, Hal and Julie continued to live quietly at their home in Auburn. Despite their newfound celebrity status,

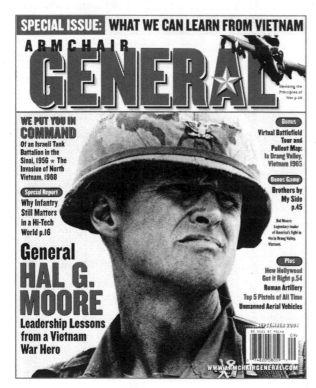

The September 2004 issue of *Armchair General* magazine, featuring a cover story on Hal Moore. It was the best-selling issue in the magazine's history.
© *Armchair General*

they remained the same devoted couple they had been for over fifty years. However, in February 2004 Julie learned that she had been stricken with "oat cell" cancer—a rare form of the disease which gave her only weeks to live. Although it was the most devastating news of their lives, Julie reacted to it with grace and composure. In her younger years, her father had said: "You are a Compton, and Comptons are thoroughbreds, and thoroughbreds don't cry." The night before she passed away, Hal, Joe, and her five children were by her bedside at the local hospice in Auburn. With as much strength as she could muster, she whispered, "Oh Joe, we've come so far together, and we still have so far to go." She died on the morning of April 18, 2004—just six weeks after her diagnosis. She was seventy-five years old.[252]

In the days following Julie's death, the family received an outpouring of condolences from across the nation. If there was ever a woman meant to be an Army spouse, it was Julie Moore. Throughout her husband's career, she had been a Girl Scout leader, a Boy Scout den mother, volunteered for the Red Cross, comforted war widows, and was instrumental in setting up the Army Community Service programs which have since become a staple of Army life.

On the morning of her funeral, April 22, 2004, the Catholic church in Auburn overflowed with mourners. In a powerful and moving eulogy, her son Greg said: "Her gracefulness ensured that she could never turn away when she sensed others suffering. In this compassion, in this, was the breath of God. It fell closely on so many." The mile-long funeral procession then made its way to the gates of the Fort Benning cemetery where Julie was laid to rest. "There were generals and colonels and a former governor of Alabama there to see her off," Moore said. "There were former sergeants and former specialists and former privates, and there were some of the widows and children of men whose funerals she had attended in the same cemetery so many years before."[253]

As of this writing (2013), Hal Moore continues to reside in Auburn, Alabama. "When I think of my Julie, which is every single day, I think of what it says in the Bible, Proverbs 31:10-12: 'A good wife is far more precious than jewels. The heart of her husband trusts in her and he will have no lack of gain. She brings him good and not harm, all the days of her life." Now, whenever Moore returns home from a trip, or even a small outing in the local town, he opens the front door and says, "Julie, I'm home," even though she's no longer there to greet him.[254]

Moore paying his respects to his beloved wife Julie at the Fort Benning
Cemetary. *Photo courtesy of Toby Warren*

Since Julie's passing, he often visits her at the Fort Benning cemetery—
a place which she often referred to as "Holy Mother Army." As he walks
through the garden of white tombstones, he communes in silent reverence
with his wife and his fallen troops, waiting for the day when he will be reunited with them once again.

EPILOGUE: A LIFE IN WORDS

"The American soldier, he is the best fighting man that I have ever seen . . . and I would like for you, if you convey anything out of this area where we've been for the last three days and nights, please convey to the American people what a tremendous fighting man we have here. He's courageous, he's aggressive, and he's kind. And he'll go where you tell him to go. And he's got self-discipline. And he's got good unit discipline. He's just an outstanding man, and having commanded this battalion for eighteen months [pauses] . . . you must excuse my emotions here . . . but when I see some of these men go out the way that they have [pauses again] . . . I can't tell you how highly I feel for them. They're tremendous."
—*News interview with Hal Moore at LZ X-Ray following the Battle of Ia Drang*

"In the game of baseball, three strikes and you're out. But in the game of life, three strikes and you're *not* out. There's always one more thing you can do to influence the outcome of any situation you're in."

"There are two things a leader can do: he can either contaminate his environment with his attitudes and actions, or he can inspire confidence. He must be visible on the battlefield; he must be in the battle, battalion commander on down—brigade and division commander on occasion. He must exhibit his determination to prevail no matter what the odds or how desperate the situation. He must have and display the will to win by his actions, his words, the tone of his voice on the radio and face-to-face, his appearance, his demeanor, his countenance, the look in his eyes. He must remain calm and cool—no fear. He must ignore the dust, the noise, the smoke, the explosions, the screams of the wounded, the yells, or the dead lying around him—that is all normal. He must never give off any hint or evidence that he is uncertain about a positive outcome, even in the most desperate situations."

"In battle, a leader must ask himself: 'What am I doing that I should not be doing?' and 'What am I *not* doing that I should be doing?' If nothing's wrong, then there's nothing wrong *except* that there's nothing wrong. That's exactly when a leader must be most alert."

"Learn to trust your instincts. In critical and fast-moving battlefield situations, your instincts and intuition amount to an instant estimate of the situation. Your instincts are the product of your education, your reading, your personality, and your experience—trust your instincts. When seconds count, instincts and decisiveness come into play. Let's not second-guess the decision; make it happen. In the process, you cannot stand around slack-jawed when hit with the unexpected. He must face up to the facts, deal with them, and move on."

"Prepare your unit for your death and for the loss of your next in command, and so on through the organization. At every level, the soldier must know how to take over for every person he reports to."

"Troops perform well in combat when they have received stressful, realistic training; rigorous physical conditioning; and stern, fair and square discipline. It is equally important to meet their personal needs including food, water, mail and information about what is going on and why."

"Soldiers in battle do not fight for what some leader says on television or in a speech. Soldiers fight and die for their buddies. They do not want to let their buddies down. It's a matter of honor."

"Be dead honest and totally candid with those above and below you."

"There must be total loyalty, up *and* down the chain of command."

"If you have to take a subordinate to the woodshed, do it in private. Praise someone in public; correct or council him privately. Never take a subordinate's pride or self-respect away."

"Treat everyone fair and square, without favorites. If you discover subordinates with extraordinary talents, give them the toughest jobs, not the easiest ones, and mentor them."

"Stay away from higher headquarters or corporate headquarters unless summoned. No good can come of wandering aimlessly around corridors filled with bosses alert for any sign that someone is underemployed."

"As you push power and decision-making authority down, you must also push subsequent praise and recognition for outstanding unit performance down as well. Don't hog the glory for yourself if you want to build a superb team."

"Good leaders don't wait for official permission to try out a new idea. In any organization, if you go looking for permission, you will inevitably find the one person who thinks his job is to say 'No!' It's easier to get forgiveness than permission."

"The leader in the field is always right and the rear echelon wrong, unless proven otherwise. Shift power and accountability to the people who are bringing in the beans, not the ones who are counting or analyzing them."

"Love is not a word military leaders throw around easily but it is the truth as I know it. Especially if you are a military leader. You must love what you are doing, because the rewards are few and the risks and hardships are many. You must love the soldiers who serve under you, for you will ask everything of them, up to and including their precious lives."

"Know the enemy; know yourself. You will win a thousand battles."

MOORE'S CITATION FOR THE DISTINGUISHED SERVICE CROSS

HEADQUARTERS
UNITED STATES ARMY, PACIFIC
APO San Francisco 96558
GENERAL ORDERS / 1 June 1966
NUMBER 126
AWARD OF THE DISTINGUISHED SERVICE CROSS

TC 320. The following AWARD is announced.
MOORE, HAROLD G JR. 027678 COLONEL Infantry United States Army
Awarded: Distinguished Service Cross
Date action: 14 through 16 November 1965
Theater: Not applicable

Reason: For extraordinary heroism in connection with military operations against an armed hostile force in the Republic of Vietnam. During the period 14 through 16 November 1965, Colonel Moore (then Lieutenant Colonel), Commanding Officer, 1st Battalion, 7th Cavalry, 1st Cavalry Division (Airmobile), was participating with his unit in a vital search and destroy operation in the Ia Drang Valley, Republic of Vietnam. Upon entering the landing zone with the first rifle company, Colonel Moore personally commenced the firefight to gain control of the zone by placing accurate fire upon the Viet Cong from an exposed position in his hovering helicopter.

Throughout the initial assault phase, Colonel Moore repeatedly exposed himself to intense hostile fire to insure the proper and expedient deployment of friendly troops. By his constant movement and repeated exposure to this insurgent fire, Colonel Moore, with complete disregard for his own personal safety, set the standard for his combat troops by a courageous display of "leadership by example" which characterized all his actions throughout the long and deadly battle. Inspired by his constant presence and active participation against the overwhelming insurgent hordes, the friendly forces solidified their perimeter defenses and repulsed numerous Viet Cong assaults.

On 15 November 1965, the embattled battalion was again attacked by a three-pronged insurgent assault aimed at surrounding and destroying the friendly forces in one great advance. With great skill and foresight, Colonel Moore moved from position to position, directing accurate fire and giving moral support to the defending forces. By his successful predictions of insurgent attack plans, he was able to thwart all their efforts by directing barrages of small arms, mortar, and artillery fire in conjunction with devastating air strikes against Viet Cong positions and attack zones. As the grueling battle continued into the third day, another large Viet Cong strike was repulsed through Colonel Moore's ability to shift men and firepower at a moment's notice against the savage, last-ditch efforts of the insurgents to break through the friendly positions. Colonel Moore's battalion, inspired by his superb leadership, combat participation, and moral support, finally decimated the well-trained and numerically superior Viet Cong force so decidedly that they withdrew in defeat, leaving over 800 of their dead on the battlefield, and resulting in a great victory for the 1st Battalion.

Colonel Moore's extraordinary heroism and gallantry in action were in keeping with the highest traditions of the United States Army and reflect great credit upon himself and the military service.

Authority: By direction of the President, under the provisions of the Act of Congress, approved 25 July 1963; Department of the Army Message 323747, 12 December 1962, as amended; and Department of the Army Message 702316, 3 February 1965.

Special instructions: This award supersedes the award of the Silver Star to Lieutenant Colonel Harold G. Moore, Jr., for gallantry in action during the period 14 to 16 November 1965 as announced in General Orders Number 1701) Headquarters, United States Army, Vietnam, dated 18 March 1966.

NOTES

CHAPTER 1

1 Interview with Lieutenant General (ret.) Harold G. Moore, November 14, 2010.

2 Warren, Toby (aka "Hal Moore's Driver"). *A General's Spiritual Journey*, p.5. Hereafter referred to as "Driver."

3 Interview with Hal Moore, November 14, 2010; *We Are Soldiers Still*, p.158.

4 Ibid.

5 Ibid.

6 Interview with Hal Moore, November 14, 2010; *We Are Soldiers Still*, p.159.

7 Ibid.

8 Moore later noted the irony of gaining an appointment from Georgia and having never set foot in the state.

9 *We Are Soldiers Still*, p.73.

10 Moore, Hal. "My Chronicle," p.2, appearing in *Class Autobiographies*. Class of 1945 Special Publications, West Point AOG. Hereafter referred to as "My Chronicle."

11 Moore, *USMA Fifty Year Book*. Class of 1945 Special Publications, West Point AOG. Hereafter referred to as *Fifty Year Book*.

12 Interview with Lieutenant General (ret.) Harold G. Moore, November 14, 2010; "My Chronicle," p.2; *We Are Soldiers Still*, p.73.

13 *Fifty Year Book*.

14 Interview with Lieutenant General (ret.) Harold G. Moore, November 14, 2010; *Fifty Year Book*.

15 Camp Popolopen has since been renamed Camp Buckner. Its original name came from the nearby Lake Popolopen, one of several landmarks within the Hudson Highlands range.

16 Interview with Lieutenant General (ret.) Harold G. Moore, November 14, 2010; *Fifty Year Book*.

17 *Fifty Year Book*; Driver, p.8.

CHAPTER 2

18 *We Are Soldiers Still*, p.192; Interviews with Hal Moore, December 12, 2010 and August 11, 2011.

19 Interview with Lieutenant General (ret.) Harold G. Moore, August 11, 2011.

20 Ibid; Kochak, Jacque. "A General's Spiritual Journey," *The Auburn Villager*, May 16, 2008.

21 Flanagan, EM. *The Angels: A History of the 11th Airborne Division*, p. 379.

22 Ibid, p.382.

23 Interviews with Hal Moore, December 12, 2010 and August 11, 2011.

24 Ibid.

25 Ibid.

26 Ibid.

27 Ibid.

28 Ibid.

29 Ibid.

30 Ibid.

31 Ibid.

32 Ibid.

33 Waters, Christopher W. Quoting Hal Moore in "Lt. General Harold G. Moore: A Study in Battle Command," Waters' graduation thesis at the Air Command and Staff College, Maxwell AFB, p. 18.

34 Ibid.

35 Interview with Lieutenant General (ret.) Harold G. Moore, August 12, 2011.

36 *We Are Soldiers Still*, p.217.

37 Ibid.

38 Waters, 19.

39 Ibid, 20.

40 Interview with Lieutenant General (ret.) Harold G. Moore, August 12, 2011.

41 Ibid.

42 Moore, Hal. Groom letter to *Fayetteville Observer*; original typed letter in Moore's possession; November 1949. As a humorous aside, Colonel Compton, a devoted artillery officer, was initially mortified that his daughter wanted to marry an infantryman. The infantry and artillery branches have had a long-standing rivalry within the US Army. In protest of his daughter's engagement, Colonel Compton purportedly locked himself in their home's basement during the engagement party. While the guests were upstairs enjoying the party, the heretofore tee-totaling Colonel Compton drank away his sorrows in the basement. Shortly thereafter, however, Compton took a strong liking to Hal and treated him as a full member of the family.

CHAPTER 3

43 Blumenson, Martin. "Lessons Learned: Reviewing the Korean War." *Army Magazine*, July 2010, p. 60.

44 Driver, p. 5.

45 Interview with Lieutenant General (ret.) Harold G. Moore, August 12, 2011.

46 *We Are Soldiers Still*, p.217; Interview with Lieutenant General (ret.) Harold G. Moore, December 12, 2010.

47 Moore, "My Chronicle," p. 2.

48 Hal Moore letter to Julie, June 1952.

49 Ibid, June 19, 1952.

50 Ibid, June 25, 1952; Interview with Lieutenant General (ret.) Harold G. Moore, February 4, 2011.

51 Ibid.

52 Ibid, June 27–July 6, 1952.

53 Ibid, July 6, 1952.

54 Ibid

55 Ibid, July 10, 1952.

56 Ibid.

57 Ibid, August 13, 1952.

58 Ibid, August 19, 1952.

59 Ibid, October 3, 1952.

60 Ibid, October 18, 1952.

61 Ibid, October 18-24, 1952.

62 Ibid, October 24, 1952.

63 Ibid, November 14, 1952.

64 Interview with Lieutenant Colonel (ret.) Steve Moore, October 10, 2012.

65 Ibid, January 17, 1953.

66 Ibid, January 31, 1953; Interview with Lieutenant General (ret.) Harold G. Moore, February 4, 2011.

67 Ibid, February 2, 1953.

68 Ibid, February 7, 1953.

69 Ibid.

70 Ibid, February 17, 1953.

71 Ibid, February 24, 1953.

72 Ibid, March 3, 1953; Interview with Lieutenant General (ret.) Harold G. Moore, February 4, 2011.

73 Ibid, March 30, 1953.

74 Ibid; Interview with Lieutenant General (ret.) Harold G. Moore, February 4, 2011.

75 Ibid, April 7, 1953.

76 Interview with Lieutenant General (ret.) Harold G. Moore, February 4, 2011.

77 McWilliams, *On Hallowed Ground: The Last Battle for Pork Chop Hill*, p.430-435.

CHAPTER 4

78 Interview with Lieutenant General (ret.) Harold G. Moore, August 12, 2011; Schwarzkopf, Introduction to *We Are Soldiers Still*

79 Elkey, James. "My Chronicle," p. 3, appearing in *Class Autobiographies*. Class of 1945 Special Publications, West Point AOG.

80 Panel Discussion with Hal Moore and Joe Galloway, "On: We Are Soldiers Still," September 17, 2008.

81 *We Are Soldiers Still*, 181; "My Chronicle," p.3.

82 "My Chronicle," p. 3; Moore, *We Were Soldiers Once . . . and Young*, p. 10.

83 Johnson, *Winged Sabers*, p. 2.

84 Interview with Lieutenant General (ret.) Harold G. Moore, August 12, 2011; "My Chronicle," p. 3.

85 Interview with Lieutenant Colonel (ret.) Steve Moore, October 20, 2012.

86 Ibid.

87 *We Were Soldiers Once . . . and Young*, p. 11.

88 Ibid, p.12.

89 Ibid.

90 Ibid, p.13.

91 Ibid, p.17.

92 Ibid, p.18.

93 Ibid.

94 *We Are Soldiers Still*, p. 74-75.

95 Ibid; *We Were Soldiers Once . . . and Young*, p. 19.

96 Interview with Lieutenant General (ret.) Harold G. Moore, August 12, 2011.

97 *We Were Soldiers Once . . . and Young*, p. 19.

98 Panzera, David. "Foundations of Faith," p. 14. A biographical thesis submitted for graduation from the Air Command and Staff College, Maxwell AFB.

99 Ibid, p.15.

100 *We Were Soldiers Once . . . and Young*, p. 24.

101 Ibid.

102 Ibid, p.25.

103 Ibid.

104 Ibid.

105 Ibid, p.13.

106 Ibid.

107 Ibid, p.14.

108 Ibid, p.14-15.

109 Ibid, p.16.

110 Ibid, p.26.

111 Ibid.

112 Interview with Ballard Moore, August 4, 2012.

CHAPTER 5

113 *We Were Soldiers Once . . . and Young*, p. 27

114 Ibid.

115 Ibid.
116 Ibid, p.28.
117 Ibid.
118 Ibid.
119 Ibid, p.29.
120 Ibid, p.30.
121 Ibid, p.31.
122 Ibid, p.32.
123 Ibid, p.33; Panel Discussion with Hal Moore at the American Veterans Center, November 7, 2008. Hereafter referred to as "Hal Moore Panel Discussion, November 7, 2008."
124 Ibid, p.34.
125 Ibid; "Hal Moore Panel Discussion, November 7, 2008."
126 Ibid, p.35; "Hal Moore Panel Discussion, November 7, 2008."
127 Ibid, p.38.
128 Ibid, p.39.
129 Ibid.
130 Ibid, p.40.
131 Ibid, p.41.
132 Ibid, p.43.
133 Ibid, p.44.
134 Ibid, p.59.
135 Ibid, p.60.
136 Ibid.
137 Ibid, p.61.
138 Ibid, p.64.
139 Ibid, p.65.
140 Ibid.
141 Cash, *Seven Firefights in Vietnam*, p.12.
142 *We Were Soldiers Once . . . And Young*, p.67.
143 Ibid, p.68.
144 Ibid.
145 Ibid, p.69.
146 Ibid, p.70–73.
147 Ibid, p.73–74.
148 Ibid, p.75.
149 Ibid, p.77.
150 Ibid, p.78; "Hal Moore Panel Discussion, November 7, 2008."
151 Ibid, p.79.
152 Ibid, p.87; Cash, p.15.
153 Ibid, p.104; Cash, p.17.
154 Ibid, p. 140.

155 Ibid, p.135.
156 Panel discussion with Hal Moore at the American Veterans Center, November 7, 2008.
157 Ibid.
158 Ibid, p.129.
159 Ibid, p.143.
160 Ibid, p.161.
161 Ibid, p.175.
162 Ibid, p.176. Nakayama's daughter had actually been born on November 7, 1965 but
    he had not been informed of the early delivery. Her anticipated due date was Novem-
    ber 15. Nakayama had been a lieutenant in the Idaho National Guard, but when he
    entered active duty, he took the brevet rank of PFC while waiting for his regular com-
    mission to come through.
163 Ibid, p.177.
164 Ibid, p.180. Rescorla was a British immigrant who joined the US Army after seeing
    several American GIs throughout his hometown in the UK during World War II.
    After the war, Rescorla continued to serve in the Army Reserve and attained the rank
    of Colonel. As a civilian, he worked as the Director of Security for Morgan Stanley in
    New York City. Rick Rescorla tragically perished at the World Trade Center in the
    terrorist attacks on September 11, 2001.
165 Ibid, p.180.
166 Ibid, p.184; Cash, p.34-36.
167 Ibid, p.195.
168 Ibid, p.205.
169 Ibid, p.216.
170 Ibid, p.218.
171 Ibid, p.345.
172 Ibid; p.346.
173 Ibid, p.367.
174 Ibid, p.368.
175 Ibid, p.370.
176 Ibid.
177 Ibid, p.370-71.

CHAPTER 6
178 Stanton, *The 1st Cav in Vietnam: Anatomy of a Division*, p.69.
179 Moore, "After-Action Report: Operation Masher/White Wing, 25 Jan–3 Feb 1966."
    Hereafter referred to as "Masher/White Wing."
180 Ibid.
181 Stanton, p.71.
182 "Masher/White Wing," p.2
183 Ibid.
184 Stanton, p.73.

185 Ibid; "Masher/White Wing," p.4-6.
186 Ibid; "People," TIME Magazine, March 11, 1966.
187 Ibid.
188 Moore, "After Action Report: Operation Davy Crockett," p.3.
189 Ibid.
190 *We Were Soldiers Once . . . and Young*, p.372.
191 Ibid, p.373.
192 Ibid.
193 Ibid.

CHAPTER 7
194 *We Are Soldiers Still*, p.219.
195 *We Were Soldiers Once . . . and Young*, p.351.
196 Ibid, p.352.
197 Ibid.
198 "My Chronicle," p.3.
199 Stewart, *American Military History Volume II: The United States Army in a Global Era, 1917-2003*, p.333.
200 Interview with Lieutenant General (ret.) Harold G. Moore, August 13, 2011; Panel Discussion with Hal Moore at the American Veterans Center, November 8, 2008; *We Are Soldiers Still*, p.173.
201 Ibid.
202 Ibid.
203 *We Are Soldiers Still*, p.174.
204 Panel Discussion with Hal Moore at the American Veterans Center, November 8, 2008.
205 Ibid.
206 Ibid.
207 *We Are Soldiers Still*, p.176.
208 Ibid, p.177.
209 Moore, "7th Division Equal Opportunity Policy." Original copy in Moore's possession.
210 Interview with Lieutenant General (ret.) Harold G. Moore, August 13, 2011; Panel Discussion with Hal Moore at the American Veterans Center, November 8, 2008.
211 Ibid; *We Are Soldiers Still*, p.178.
212 Galloway, Letter to Hal Moore dated March 26, 1971.
213 Moore, *Building a Volunteer Army: The Fort Ord Contribution*, p.97-98. Hereafter referred to as *Building a Volunteer Army*.
214 Ibid, p.99.
215 Ibid, p.102.
216 Ibid, p.102-103.
217 Interview with Lieutenant General (ret.) Harold G. Moore, August 13, 2011; *We Are Soldiers Still*, p.179.

218 *We Are Soldiers Still*, p.179-80.

219 Ibid; *Building a Volunteer Army*, p.117.

220 *Building a Volunteer Army*, p.116.

221 Ibid.

222 Interview with Lieutenant General (ret.) Harold G. Moore, August 13, 2011.

223 "Moore Testifies on Hill: Combat Arms Bonus Need Stressed," *Army Times*, May 7, 1975.

224 "My Chronicle," p.4.

225 Ibid.

CHAPTER 8

226 *We Are Soldiers Still*, p.14.

227 Ibid, p.14–15.

228 Moore, "Memories of Men and Mountains: Russia, September 1989," p.1.

229 Ibid.

230 Ibid.

231 Ibid.

232 Ibid, p.2.

233 Ibid.

234 Ibid, p.3.

235 Ibid, p.5.

236 Ibid, p.4.

237 Ibid, p.5.

238 *We Are Soldiers Still*, p.220.

239 Ibid, p.17.

240 Ibid, p.29.

241 Ibid, p.2.

242 Ibid, p.48.

243 Ibid, p.51.

244 Ibid, p.60.

245 Ibid, p.84.

246 Ibid, p.88.

247 Ibid, p.92.

248 Ibid.

249 Ibid, p.98.

250 Ibid, p.111.

251 Interview with Lieutenant General (ret.) Harold G. Moore, August 13, 2011; *We Are Soldiers Still*, p.222.

252 *We Are Soldiers Still*, p.223-24.

253 Ibid.

254 Ibid; Interview with Lieutenant General (ret.) Harold G. Moore, August 13, 2011.

BIBLIOGRAPHY

PRIMARY SOURCES

AUTHOR INTERVIEWS:
Interview with Pike Conway, June 23, 2012.
Interview with Ballard Moore, August 4, 2012.
Interview with Bill Moore, June 22, 2012.
Interview with Lieutenant General (ret.) Harold G. Moore, November 14, 2010.
Interview with Lieutenant General (ret.) Harold G. Moore, December 12, 2010.
Interview with Lieutenant General (ret.) Harold G. Moore, February 4, 2011.
Interview with Lieutenant General (ret.) Harold G. Moore, August 11, 2011.
Interview with Lieutenant General (ret.) Harold G. Moore, August 12, 2011.
Interview with Lieutenant General (ret.) Harold G. Moore, August 13, 2011.
Interview with Lieutenant Colonel (ret.) Steve Moore, October 10, 2012.
Interview with Lieutenant Colonel (ret.) Steve Moore, October 20, 2012.
Interview with Bill Walls, June 22, 2012.

ARCHIVAL MATERIAL:
American Veterans Center
> *2007 American Veterans Center Annual Conference.* November 8–10, 2007. Video footage of the 2007 panel discussion featuring Harold G. Moore, Joseph Galloway, and Ramon "Tony" Nadal.
> *2008 American Veterans Center Annual Conference.* November 6–8, 2008. Video footage of the 2008 panel discussion featuring Harold G. Moore, Joseph Galloway, and Ramon "Tony" Nadal.
> The Hal Moore Collection. Various photographs, correspondence, and personal papers spanning the years 1942–2002.

Pritzker Military Library
"Joe Galloway and Hal Moore: We Are Soldiers Still." Interview video footage. September 17, 2008.
"Front and Center: We Were Soldiers Once . . . and Young." Interview footage with Hal Moore and Joe Galloway. October 8, 2005.

St. Joseph's Prep Alumni Association
St. Joseph's Photographic Collection, 1935–1968

Texas Tech University–Vietnam Studies Center
Verrone, Richard. "Interview with Harold G. Moore." November 10, 2005. Video footage of interview.

United States Army Military History Institute
Moore, Harold G. "Statement by Lieutenant General H.G. Moore, Deputy Chief of Staff for Personnel, US Army, before the Subcommittee on Manpower and Personnel, Committee on Armed Services, US Senate: Manpower Management and Requirements." Government Printing Office: Washington, DC, 1977.
Moore, Harold G. "After Action Report: Operation Davy Crockett." APO San Francisco, Headquarters, 3rd Brigade, 1st Cavalry Division, 1966.
Moore, Harold G. "After Action Report: Operation Hop Out." APO US Forces 96490: Headquarters, 1st Battalion, 7th Cavalry, 1965.

United States Military Academy Association of Graduates.
Class of 1945 Special Publications
Cadet Days. United States Military Academy: New York, 2000.
Elkey, James H. "My Chronicle," in Class Autobiographies. United States Military Academy: New York, 2000.
Moore, Harold G. "My Chronicle," in Class Autobiographies. United States Military Academy: New York, 2000.
Moore, Harold G. "Citation for the Distinguished Service Cross," in Special Items. United States Military Academy: New York, 2000.
USMA Fifty Year Book, 1945–1995. United States Military Academy: New York, 1995.

PUBLISHED MATERIAL:
Moore, Harold G. Building a Volunteer Army: The Fort Ord Contribution. US Army Center of Military History: Washington, DC, 1975.

Moore, Harold G. and Joseph Galloway. *We Were Soldiers Once . . . and Young*. Random House: New York, 1992.

Moore, Harold G. and Joseph Galloway. *We Are Soldiers Still*. Harper Collins: New York, 2008.

SECONDARY SOURCES:

Appleman, Roy E. *South to Naktong, North to the Yalu*. Army Center for Military History: Washington, DC, 1992.

Blumenson, Martin. "Lessons Learned: Reviewing the Korean War." *Army Magazine*, July 2010.

Burke, GG. "Hal Moore: Is He the Blood-and-Guts General Patton We Need in Vietnam?" *MALE Magazine, June 1966*.

Cash, John A. *Seven Firefights in Vietnam*. Army Center of Military History: Washington, DC, 1985.

Kochak, Jacque. "A General's Spiritual Journey," *The Auburn Villager*, May 16, 2008.

Fehrenbach, TR. *This Kind of War*. Potomac Books: Dulles, Virginia, 2001.

Flanagan, EM. *The Angels: A History of the 11th Airborne Division*. Presidio Press: New York, 1989.

Graves, Thomas C. "Transforming the Force: The 11th Air Assault Division (Test) from 1963-1965." School of Advanced Military Studies, Army Command and General Staff College: Fort Leavenworth, Kansas, 2000.

Hermes, Walter J. *United States Army in the Korean War: Truce Tent and Fighting Front*. Army Center for Military History: Washington, DC, 1992.

Johnson, Lawrence H. *Winged Sabers: The Air Cavalry in Vietnam*. Stackpole Books: Mechanicsburg, Pennsylvania, 1990.

McWilliams, Bill. *On Hallowed Ground: The Last Battle for Pork Chop Hill*. Berkley Caliber: New York, 2004.

Mossman, Billy C. *United States Army in the Korean War: Ebb and Flow, November 1950-July 1951*. Army Center for Military History: Washington DC, 1990.

"Operation White Wing." *Time Magazine*, February 11, 1966.

Panzera, David. "Foundations of Faith: A Biography of Lieutenant General Harold G. 'Hal' Moore." Graduation thesis completed at the Air Command and Staff College, Maxwell AFB, 2007.

Sobel, Brian. "Hal G. Moore: The Legacy and Lessons of an American Warrior." *Armchair General Magazine*, September 2004.

Stanton, Shelby. *The 1st Cav in Vietnam: Anatomy of a Division*. Presidio Press: New York, 1999.

Spector, Ronald H. *Advice and Support: The Early Years, 1941–1960*. Army Center for Military History: Washington, DC, 1983.

Tolson, John. *Airmobility 1961–1971*. Army Center for Military History: Washington, DC, 1982.

Warren, Toby (aka "Hal Moore's Driver"). *A General's Spiritual Journey.* Wild Goose Ministries: Lake Placid, Florida, 2007.

Waters, Christopher K. "Lt. General Harold G. Moore: A Study in Battle Command." Graduation thesis completed at the Air Command and Staff College, Maxwell AFB, 2006.

INDEX